Historical Background and Literary Periods

TEACHER'S EDITION

McDougal Littell

THE LANGUAGE OF
LITERATURE

AMERICAN LITERATURE

- Readings and Activities for each Historical and Literary Period
- Notetaking Guides
- Graphic Organizers
- Additional Assessment Questions with Answer Key

McDougal Littell
A DIVISION OF HOUGHTON MIFFLIN COMPANY

To the Teacher

American Literature: Historical Background and Literary Periods provides practice for the critical skill of note taking. The guide begins with student-friendly instruction about note taking, pointing out ways to approach different texts and to use appropriate graphic organizers with those texts. The booklet provides challenging literary articles to give students the opportunity to learn more about the historical period, the literary movements, and the political structures of the societies that produced the literature in their student texts. The booklet also includes primary sources set off in boxes. These sources not only add interest but also serve as a bridge for students' note taking, allowing them the chance to apply what they have learned to authentic literature. To encourage practice, each article is bordered by space for student note taking, and appropriate graphic organizers appear throughout to facilitate students' work.

ISBN-13: 978-0-618-69192-0   ISBN-10: 0-618-69192-8

3 4 5 6 7 8 9—MDO—09 08 07 06

Contents

∽ Notes

_____

_____

_____

_____

_____

_____

_____

_____

_____

_____

_____

_____

_____

_____

_____

_____

_____

_____

_____

Note Taking

Why We Do It

Whether they take the form of a few words jotted down on scrap paper or a formal outline, notes are an invaluable tool for review or study because they remind you of what was important in the text and help you make sense of complex ideas.

Think, for instance, of William Bradford's _History of Plymouth Plantation_ (page 29). It's written in English but was composed in a time where syntax, spelling, and other elements differed from our modern-day English. Taking notes and restating the contents of this letter in your own words would clarify the meaning of the unfamiliar vocabulary and complex ideas contained in this difficult text.

Or think of an article concerning a historical event. Taking notes and breaking down the contents into smaller parts would help you sort out events and details in your own mind.

In order to take the right kinds of notes, ask yourself what sort of material you are dealing with and what you will need your notes for. A movie review will require less attention to detail than an article about history. Are you recording information to use in a research paper? Clarifying information from a difficult article? Recording important points made in a class discussion for later review? Or are you trying to keep characters and events straight in a fictional text? But even though the form of note taking you use depends on your purpose for taking the notes and on the type of material you are working with, the same analytical skills are needed.

How We Do It

Identify and Summarize   A well-structured essay or article will introduce its main idea—its big topic—right at the beginning. This is called the _topic sentence_. Every paragraph that follows will then carry that main idea into greater and greater levels of detail.

Your first task is to *identify* the main ideas or events and their supporting details. This is the backbone of your note taking. After identifying the main ideas, you *summarize,* or restate them in your own words. Summarizing helps you clarify dense and complicated passages. The purpose of the process is to extract the most important points and condense the information into its most basic form. Identifying and summarizing main ideas are the key to successful note taking. It is important to understand a work's organization because it will determine how you should best organize your notes.

Try to make your notes clear and brief. Your restatements of the main ideas must accurately capture the ideas presented in the text. If you make your statements too short, you won't understand them later. If you include too much information, it will be difficult to identify the ideas you thought were most important.

Apply these skills of identifying and summarizing to the following excerpt from "In Harmony with Nature" found on page 13 of this booklet.

> Although traditional Native American literature has many forms and functions, much of it emphasizes the importance of living in harmony with the natural world. In Native American belief, human beings have a kinship with animals, plants, the land, heavenly bodies, and the elements. All of these things are seen as alive and aware. Furthermore, the human and nonhuman are seen as parts of a sacred whole.

How could you summarize the main idea of this passage in your own words? One way to do this would be to write: "All forms of Native American literature present a central message of respecting the natural world."

Outline   Outlines can be formal or informal. *Formal outlines* arrange the main points in a very systematic form. *Informal outlines* organize the main points in any way the writer finds convenient.

_____

_____

_____

_____

_____

_____

Example of a Formal Outline

I. Getting into college requires
   A. Time
      1. Conduct background research
      2. Gather paperwork
   B. Money
      1. Financial aid
      2. Application fees

_____

_____

_____

_____

_____

_____

_____

_____

Take this example:

> It takes time and money to gain entrance into the right college. First, you must conduct background research on the institution that will best suit your needs. Then, you must gather and complete the needed paperwork, not only to gain admission, but also to apply for financial aid. Finally, you must send in your completed paperwork along with your application fees.

Here the main idea is directly stated in the first sentence: to get into the right college you need time and money. The sentences that follow are the supporting details: what they say supports the main idea. A formal outline of this paragraph might look something like the one on the left. Notice that in the formal outline all the categorical levels are arranged in a hierarchy, with at least two points under each category.

But main ideas are not always stated so directly. You may need to use your critical thinking skills to find them. Try this example:

> To gain entrance into the right college for you, you must conduct background research on the institution that will best suit your needs. Then, you must gather and complete the needed paperwork not only to gain admission but also to apply for financial aid. Finally, you must send in your completed paperwork along with your application fees.

Both examples have the same main idea but the second one is not as direct. Only after you read the supporting details can you infer what the author is saying.

Usually, an entire essay will consist of more than one main idea. Your note taking should identify and summarize each idea, one by one. At the end, all your summaries should build upon each other in support of the "big idea."

Tools of the Trade

Depending on the complexity of your material and on the purpose for which you are taking notes, there are different ways to break down and summarize a text. *Graphic organizers* are visual formats that serve as the basic tools for organizing notes. Graphic organizers enable you to clearly review relationships among ideas or events and improve your understanding and retention of fictional and non-fictional material. After you have identified and summarized the main ideas of the text you are reading, you will be able to determine which type of graphic organizer will work best for you.

Graphic Organizers   You may already be familiar with some graphic organizers. Graphic organizers such as Venn diagrams, cluster diagrams, causal chains, story maps, comparison-and-contrast charts, time lines, KWL charts, and others are visual formats that serve as the basic tools for organizing notes.

∽ Notes

_____

_____

_____

_____

_____

_____

_____

_____

KWL Chart

K What I *Know*	W What I *Want* To Learn	L What I Have *Learned*

Cluster Diagram

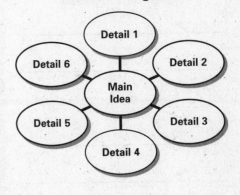

Venn Diagram

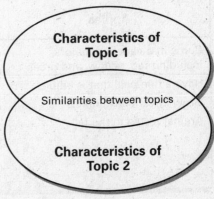

Timeline

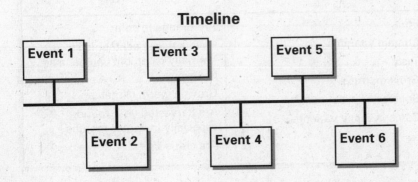

_____

_____

_____

_____

_____

_____

_____

_____

_____

_____

_____

Text Features   In nonfictional material, such as essays, articles, and textbooks, it is easy to see how a text is organized. Look for features such as titles, tables of contents, headings, subheadings, and graphic organizers. The writer uses such features to organize information and so can you. For example, look at the headings in this section. You can see that various kinds of organization will be explored topic by topic. As a reader, you can use these text features to prepare for the information you are about to encounter and determine what type of note-taking strategy to use.

Use the Right Tool!

In general, your note taking should have the same kind of organization the text itself has. For instance, a historical text is best organized along a time line or a causal chain. A fictional text, which is not as linear, is better organized as a sequence-of-events chart.

Compare and Contrast   Depending on their subject matter, other articles may organize their presentation to *compare and contrast*. An efficient way to do that is a three-column comparison-and-contrast chart like the one below that compares and contrasts apples and oranges. A Venn diagram, such as the one on page 21 of this booklet, is also a useful tool for showing such relationships.

In a chart like the one shown below you record qualities of topic A in the first column, qualities of topic B in the last column, and the similarities of both topics in the middle column.

Comparison and Contrast Chart

Apples	Similarities	Oranges
Come in a variety of colors, including red, yellow, and green Have a thin peel that is edible Grow in various climates Are harvested in the fall	Fruit Contain vitamins Tasty Grow on trees Sources of juice Come in many varieties	Are orange in color Have a thick peel that isn't normally eaten but can be used to season Grow in warm climates Are harvested year round, especially in winter months Are citrus fruits

Cause and Effect Chart of Spanish Exploration of the New World

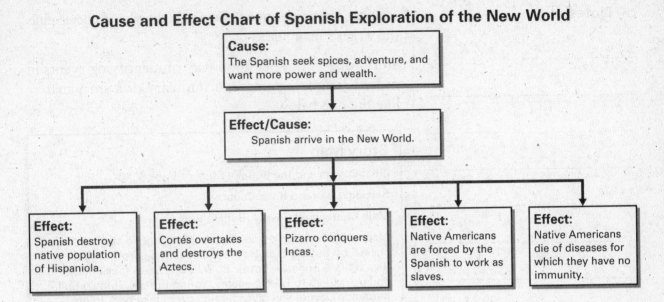

Cause:
The Spanish seek spices, adventure, and want more power and wealth.

Effect/Cause:
Spanish arrive in the New World.

Effect:
Spanish destroy native population of Hispaniola.

Effect:
Cortés overtakes and destroys the Aztecs.

Effect:
Pizarro conquers Incas.

Effect:
Native Americans are forced by the Spanish to work as slaves.

Effect:
Native Americans die of diseases for which they have no immunity.

Cause and Effect Look at the causal chain above. It maps the *causes and effects* in the fourth paragraph of "Exploration and Its Effects" on page 26 of this booklet. The pattern is that of cause-and-effect relationships. Your notes could take the form of a causal chain. Keep in mind when gathering information about historical events, it is important to not oversimplify causal relationships. Usually there is more than one cause of an event and more than one effect.

Chronological Order Most films and books occur in chronological order—that is, they proceed sequentially as time itself does. They lend themselves to the question "What's next?" In fictional texts the focus is often on the main *events* instead of the main *ideas*. If you had to take notes, you could organize them as a sequence-of-events chart and track events in their proper order.

Having recorded the main events of a fictional text, you can then use your notes to make inferences about the main idea of the text. In the case of "Coyote and the Another One" on page 21 of this booklet, the main idea is stated for you at the end of the selection: "Our problem is we are listening to the Farmer tell us who we are." In most instances, however, the main idea is not so

Sequence Chart for "Coyote and the Another One"

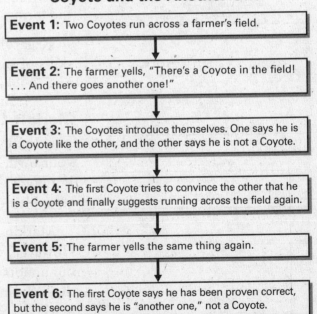

Event 1: Two Coyotes run across a farmer's field.

Event 2: The farmer yells, "There's a Coyote in the field! . . . And there goes another one!"

Event 3: The Coyotes introduce themselves. One says he is a Coyote like the other, and the other says he is not a Coyote.

Event 4: The first Coyote tries to convince the other that he is a Coyote and finally suggests running across the field again.

Event 5: The farmer yells the same thing again.

Event 6: The first Coyote says he has been proven correct, but the second says he is "another one," not a Coyote.

_____

_____

_____

_____

_____

_____

_____

_____

_____

_____

_____

_____

_____

_____

_____

_____

_____

_____

explicit. The reader must put events together to determine the writer's main idea.

Story Map Another good way of identifying events in order is a simple paragraph summary or a story map like the one below.

Story Map

Title: Coyote and the Buffalo, Student Book p. 40

Setting: Colorado River Country

Main Characters: Coyote, Buffalo Bull

Major Plot Events: Coyote disrespects a Buffalo skull and is chased by Buffalo Bull. He escapes death by promising to give Buffalo Bull new horns. Buffalo Bull takes these horns and uses them to kill his enemy, Young Buffalo. Buffalo Bull befriends Coyote and gives him a cow to take back to his people. The cow is supposed to feed them forever, as long as Coyote doesn't kill her. He gets greedy for more food than she gives, so he kills her. He not only loses the meat reward, he is also rebuffed by Buffalo Bull and sent home empty-handed.

Theme: If you behave with greed, you will get nothing in the end.

There are many other means of organization besides chronological order, cause and effect, and compare and contrast. When describing a place or a thing, a writer might use spatial order. Or, when explaining a process, a writer might use step-by-step order. As you gain experience in note taking, you will learn to adapt the form of your notes to the task at hand.

Regardless of the organization of a text, your basic skills of summarizing and outlining will always enable you to take meaningful notes.

Mark It Up!

First things first: Never mark up a book that is not your own, including textbooks and library books. If a book is yours, however, marking it up can be a valuable note-taking tool.

Marking up a text is a quick way of taking notes. However, we are not talking about merely highlighting but annotating. Start by highlighting or underlining the most important ideas you want to remember, or mark an important quotation you might want to use

The marked-up passage reads:

stream = consciousness

more to life than we know

a large knife for separating

metaphorical

collective consciousness in nature

digging into the unconscious

Time is but <u>the stream</u> I go a-fishing in. I drink at it; but while I drink I see the sandy bottom and <u>detect how shallow it is.</u> Its thin current slides away, but eternity remains. I would drink deeper; fish in the sky, whose bottom is pebbly with stars. I cannot count one. I know not the first letter of the alphabet. I have always been regretting that I was not as wise as the day I was born. The intellect is a (cleaver;) it discerns and rifts its way into the secret of things. I do not wish to be any more busy with my hands than is necessary. <u>My head is hands and feet.</u> I feel all my best faculties concentrated in it. My instinct tells me that <u>my head is an organ for burrowing,</u> as some creatures use their snout and fore paws, and with it I would mine and burrow my way through these hills. <u>I think that the richest vein is somewhere hereabouts</u>; so by the divining-rod and thin rising vapors I judge; and here I will begin to mine.

—*Walden*, by Henry David Thoreau

"rifts" - verb meaning "cuts through"

"divining rod" and "think rising vapors" - metaphorical

later. To make a mark meaningful, jot down a note in the margin. You might pull out the most important idea or write your own quick thought about it. Keep in mind that you need to be selective in your markings. If you highlight or underline nearly all of the book, your marks become meaningless. Use the marked-up text above as an example for your own practice.

Apply What You Know

You have learned what elements in a text give you clues about its structure. You have seen examples of how to break down a text into main and supporting ideas. You have practiced identifying and summarizing and have an idea of what different tools are available to convert what you take from a text into useful notes. Now apply your skills and hone your talent on the articles that follow.

∿ **Notes**

_____

_____

_____

_____

_____

_____

_____

Origins and Encounters

EVENTS IN AMERICAN LITERATURE

2000–1000 B.C.	0	A.D. 1000

1492 "Epistola," Christopher Columbus's journal describing his encounters in the New World, is published

EVENTS IN NORTH AMERICA

2000–1000 B.C.	0	A.D. 1000

c.2000–1000 B.C. Native Americans in Southwest cultivate maize, a forerunner of corn

c.400 B.C. Olmec civilization begins decline in central Mexico

c.A.D. 500 Native American tribes in Eastern woodlands establish agricultural economy and widespread trade

c.800 Mound Builder culture develops along Mississippi River (to c. 1500s)

c.1000 Anasazi build elaborate, multistory cliff dwellings in Southwest canyons (to c. 1300)

1492 Christopher Columbus sets foot in Bahamas

EVENTS IN THE WORLD

2000–1000 B.C.	0	A.D. 1000

c.1790 B.C. Hammurabi, king of Babylon, codifies set of laws

c.753 B.C. City of Rome founded

483 B.C. The Buddha dies

334 B.C. Alexander the Great begins conquest of Persia (to 323 B.C.)

c.A.D. 30 Jesus crucified

105 Chinese invent paper

c.250 Mayan civilization begins Classic Period (to c. 880)

c.476 Western Roman Empire falls

630 Prophet Muhammad conquers Mecca, which becomes holiest city of Islam

800 Charlemagne unites much of Europe and is crowned Holy Roman Emperor

1095 First of nine "holy wars," known as Crusades, begins

1206 Genghis Khan begins Mongol conquest of Asia (to 1227)

1215 In England, King John agrees to Magna Carta

c.1300 Renaissance begins in Italy

1453 Ottomans conquer Constantinople

1455 Gutenberg Bible produced on printing press

1500   **1600**

1521 Hernándo Cortés writes to king of Spain describing Aztec gifts

1527 Bartolome de la Casas begins his History of the Indians

1537 Upon returning to Spain, Álvar Núñez Cabeza de Vaca reports to Spanish king about harrowing North American journey

1588 *A Briefe and True Report of the New-Found Land of Virginia* by Thomas Harriot is published

1608 In *A True Relation of . . . Virginia*, Captain John Smith gives the first account of his capture by Algonquians

1624 Smith publishes *The General History of Virginia, New England, and the Summer Isles*, telling the story of Pocahontas

1630 Captain John Smith publishes *The True Travels, Adventures, and Observations of Captaine John Smith*

1630 William Bradford describes journey across Atlantic and Pilgrims' settlement in *Of Plymouth Plantation*

1500   **1600**

1502 Amerigo Vespucci returns from second exploration of South America and declares it a New World; the Americas are named after him

1521 Hernando Cortés conquers Aztecs and claims territory for Spain

1535 Jacques Cartier explores St. Lawrence River and claims Quebec and Montreal for France

1540 Cherokee encounter Europeans for the first time when Hernando Desoto's expedition reaches their territory

1540 Horses introduced on large scale by Spanish explorers

1607 First permanent English colony set up in Jamestown, Virginia

1618 Virginia governor Samuel Argall declares all colonists who fail to attend church will be locked in guardhouse

1619 Africans first arrive in Virginia as indentured servants

1620 Before landing at Plymouth, Pilgrims sign Mayflower Compact, establishing government by will of majority

---

1500   **1600**

1502 First enslaved Africans taken to the Americas

1517 Martin Luther begins Protestant Reformation

1522 Magellan sails around world

1526 Babur founds Mughal Empire in India

1543 Copernicus publishes theory that sun is center of universe

1588 Spanish Armada sails for England

1603 Tokugawa Ieyasu unites Japan

1613 Michael Romanov elected Russian czar, founding the Romanov dynasty

1615 Italian scientist Galileo Galilei condemned by Inquisition for supporting Copernicus's theory

In Harmony with Nature

The first American literature was created by the first people to inhabit North America—the Native Americans who were here thousands of years before Europeans arrived. The Native Americans did not think of themselves as living in a single nation as most Americans do today. Rather, the original native peoples belonged to more than 200 distinct groups, speaking more than 500 different languages. They referred to themselves by such names as *Anishinabe, Diné*, and *Lakota*—all meaning "the people" in different languages. Their ways of life, dictated by their natural surroundings, varied greatly. They had complex religious beliefs, sophisticated political systems, and strong social values, all of which were reflected in their literature.

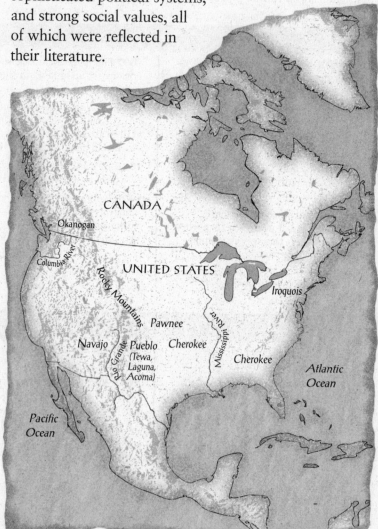

Native American literature was primarily oral, passed down from generation to generation by storytelling and performance. Some widespread types of Native American oral literature are:

- creation myths, which explain the beginning of the world;
- trickster and hero tales, which explain how the world was transformed to its present state and which express common beliefs and values of the cultures;
- ritual songs and chants, which are part of religious ceremonies.

Although traditional Native American literature has many forms and functions, much of it emphasizes the importance of living in harmony with the natural world. In Native American belief, human beings have a kinship with animals, plants, the land, heavenly bodies, and the elements. All of these things are seen as alive and aware. Furthermore, the human and nonhuman are seen as parts of a sacred whole. To Native Americans, human beings do not have dominion over nature; instead, they are part of nature and must act to maintain a right relationship with the world around them.

In Native American culture, the oral tradition was the means by which the young learned tribal history and beliefs. At the time, the Native Americans did not have a written language. The oral literature required long periods of memorization, so Native Americans often used drum music, as well as pictographs, knotted strings, and coded wampum belts as memory aids. The songs often included rhythmic repetition, which was, the people believed, how the singer communicated with animals, nature, and the world of the spirit. The rhythm and repetition also made the song easier to memorize. The young generation was able to integrate the stories into their memories because of these rhythmic techniques and the frequency with which they heard these songs. Because of the nature of the oral tradition, the literature was fluid and ever changing, unlike written records and stories.

Notes

_____

_____

_____

_____

_____

_____

_____

_____

_____

_____

_____

_____

_____

_____

_____

_____

_____

_____

As readers, you cannot experience these works as they were originally created. Instead you will read them on a page in a language different from the languages in which they were created. When you encounter creation myths, trickster tales, ritual songs, and other Native American literature, take into consideration the translation that you are reading. Even though you are an English-speaking reader and are removed from the original text on several levels, it is still possible to see the beauty and the lesson or message of the work.

Learning about the history of the cultures and the events that affected them will be instrumental in improving your understanding of the native literature. This booklet will provide information about the Cherokee culture and society to allow you to better understand how they lived before their first encounters with Europeans. You will also be introduced to the foundations of Native American literature. This introduction will provide a focus on creation myths, trickster tales, and songs.

In the last part of this booklet, the first encounters with Europeans and the effects of exploration on the native populations will be discussed. There will also be an examination of the institution of slavery as a result of colonization. Finally, you will learn more about early American literature and the origins of African American literature. Throughout this booklet, you will have the opportunity to read primary sources from various time periods and cultures.

Cherokee Nation

In the mid 1600s, about 100 years after Hernando DeSoto and his expedition encountered the first Cherokee, the Cherokee nation's population was estimated at nearly 22,500 people. The Cherokee controlled approximately 40,000 square miles of land. This area covered most of present-day Kentucky and Tennessee, as well as parts of the Carolinas, Alabama, and Georgia. The Cherokee had been around for many, many years before the arrival of the Spanish. Considering themselves to be the first and central group on Earth, they referred to themselves as "Ani-Yunwiya" (Principal People). Originally an Iroquoian people, the Cherokee split from that group and formed their own nation. When they migrated south from the Great Lakes region, they brought the Iroquoian language with them.

The Cherokee were divided into seven clans: Longhair (*Anigilohi*), Blue (*Anisahoni*), Wolf (*Aniwaya*), Wild Potato (*Anigotegewi*), Deer (*Aniawi*), Bird (*Anitsisqua*), and Paint (*Aniwodi*). A person's clan membership was determined matrilineally,

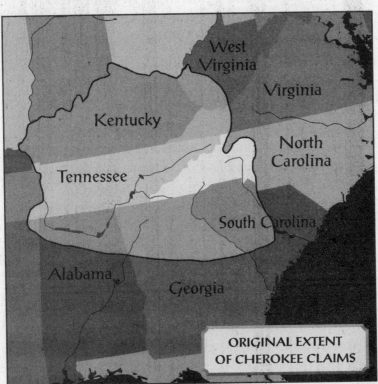

ORIGINAL EXTENT
OF CHEROKEE CLAIMS

or through the mother. Each clan consisted of several villages. Two chiefs ruled each community, a "red" chief during war and a "white" chief during peace. The Cherokee held general councils that allowed a somewhat democratic ruling process to work toward the good of the whole nation, especially when facing war with other nations.

The Cherokee held these councils in seven-sided council houses, where the seven sides represented the seven clans. Each village had such a house. In everyday living, these villages, which consisted of thirty to sixty homes, were relatively independent in ruling themselves. The tribe mainly came together during a war or to celebrate major ceremonies.

The Cherokee mostly lived in wattle-and-daub, or stick-and-mud, houses. They could build permanent structures because they were not nomadic. Their houses were partially underground and had circular frames. Later, the Cherokee would adopt log cabins as a standard abode.

An agrarian nation, the Cherokee were mostly farmers, surviving on corn, squash, and beans. They also hunted and gathered berries and other wild vegetation. The biggest annual celebration the Cherokee held was the "busk" ceremony to celebrate the harvest of corn. This ceremony included dancing, music, and games. They also held ceremonies for naming children and for electing council representatives.

The powerful and rich culture of the Cherokee thrived for hundreds of years. Unfortunately, their power was threatened when gold was found in their territory and Europeans gradually took over. Perhaps the most memorable tragedy in the history of European and Native American contact occurred in the "Trail of Tears," 1838–1839, in which thousands of Cherokee died when the U.S. Army marched them from their homeland to a reservation in Oklahoma. Nevertheless, the Cherokee traditions have been preserved in the culture and the literature. See an example of Cherokee literature on page 18 of this booklet.

Foundations of Native American Literature

Overview

When we refer to Native American literature, it is somewhat different than referring to English literature. With the exception of contemporary works, Native American literature consists mainly of written records of oral performances. These oral performances became written pieces after being translated from their native tongues into English.

Even though Native Americans come from different cultures, they have many similarities in their literary past. In general, Native Americans placed much importance on the oral tradition as these works were repositories of the peoples' histories, beliefs, entertainment, rituals, and prayers. Oral performances varied from delivering a seven-day song at a ceremonial festival to telling the equivalent of an English bedtime story. Regardless, the person passing on the oral tradition was recognized as having the power to deliver a vital message.

These translations and transcriptions of works that were originally oral can be categorized in many ways. There are tales considered to be true, which often include origin tales and creation myths. Then there are tales considered to be fictional, which express cultural values or teach a lesson. Trickster tales belong to this category. Finally, there are many varieties of songs.

No matter how the works are categorized, the Native American peoples have a rich cultural heritage that has been passed from generation to generation for thousands of years and still survives today. From these translations and transcriptions, people outside the Native American culture may glimpse the important lessons, ideas, relationships, and beliefs of these indigenous peoples of the Americas. The creation myths, trickster tales, and songs in this article will give you an overview of the scope of the Native American literary tradition.

Notes

Take notes on the selection using a cluster diagram to organize the most important information. Use a new cluster diagram for each of the sections. Doing so will help you visualize the most important characteristics of the different kinds of Native American literature.

Overview of Native American Literature

Creation Myths

Creation myths of all cultures give explanations of how the world was created. These myths aren't simple stories that are meant to be taken literally. Rather, they are explanations that address important cultural beliefs and assumptions, as well as provide answers to the big questions about life.

If you take the Cherokee creation myth, "How the World Was Made," as an example, you will see that this is no simple story. The reliance of people on animals and nature is emphasized in the tale. It also begins with a somewhat masked warning to treat the earth well because when it is "worn out," life as we know it will end.

The various Native American cultures express different beliefs, but most myths share the common theme of respecting and working with nature. In addition, many of the tales include explanations for how things came to be the way they are. Again, the Cherokee myth is a good example of this phenomenon. We learn why certain trees lose their leaves in the winter and others don't; why certain animals are nocturnal and others are not; and why the sun is positioned as it is in the sky.

These symbolic tales provide an explanation of the world and how it came into being, as well as insight into such universal questions as Who are we? How should we live? and What does this life mean?

PRIMARY SOURCE: CREATION MYTH

How the World Was Made

The earth is a great island floating in a sea of water, and suspended at each of the four cardinal points by a cord hanging down from the sky vault, which is of solid rock. When the world grows old and worn out, the people will die and the cords will break and let the earth sink down into the ocean, and all will be water again. The Indians are afraid of this.

When all was water, the animals were above in Galunlati, beyond the arch; but it was very much crowded, and they were wanting more room. They wondered what was below the water, and at last

continued on page 19

Dayunisi, "Beaver's Grandchild," the little Water-beetle, offered to go and see if it could learn. It darted in every direction over the surface of the water, but could find no firm place to rest. Then it dived to the bottom and came up with some soft mud, which began to grow and spread on every side until it became the island which we call the earth. It was afterward fastened to the sky with four cords, but no one remembers who did this.

At first the earth was flat and very soft and wet. The animals were anxious to get down, and sent out different birds to see if it was yet dry, but they found no place to alight and came back again to Galunlati. At last it seemed to be time, and they sent out the Buzzard and told him to go and make ready for them. This was the Great Buzzard, the father of all the buzzards we see now. He flew all over the earth, low down near the ground, and it was still soft. When he reached the Cherokee country, he was very tired, and his wings began to flap and strike the ground, and wherever they struck the earth there was a valley, and where they turned up again there was a mountain. When the animals above saw this, they were afraid that the whole world would be mountains, so they called him back, but the Cherokee country remains full of mountains to this day.

When the earth was dry and the animals came down, it was still dark, so they got the sun and set it in a track to go every day across the island from east to west, just overhead. It was too hot this way, and Tsiskagili, the Red Crawfish, had his shell scorched a bright red, so that his meat was spoiled; and the Cherokee do not eat it. The conjurers put the sun another hand-breadth higher in the air, but it was still too hot. They raised it another time, and another, until it was seven hand-breadths high and just under the sky

continued on page 20

_____

_____

_____

_____

_____

_____

_____

_____

_____

_____

_____

_____

_____

_____

_____

_____

_____

PRIMARY SOURCE: CREATION MYTH   *continued from page 19*

arch. Then it was right, and they left it so. This is why the conjurers call the highest place Gulkwagine Digalunlatiyun, "the seventh height," because it is above the earth. Every day the sun goes along under this arch, and returns at night on the upper side to the starting place. . . .

When the animals and plants were first made—we do not know by whom—they were told to watch and keep awake for seven nights, just as young men now fast and keep awake when they pray to their medicine. They tried to do this, and nearly all were awake through the first night, but the next night several dropped off to sleep, and the third night others were asleep, and then others, until, on the seventh night, of all the animals only the owl, the panther, and one or two more were still awake. To these were given the power to see and to go about in the dark, and to make prey of the birds and animals which must sleep at night. Of the trees only the cedar, the pine, the spruce, the holly, and the laurel were awake to the end, and to them it was given to be always green and to be greatest for medicine, but to the others it was said: "Because you have not endured to the end you shall lose your hair every winter."

Men came after the animals and plants. At first there were only a brother and sister until he struck her with a fish and told her to multiply, and so it was. In seven days a child was born to her, and thereafter every seven days another, and they increased very fast until there was danger that the world could not keep them. Then it was made that a woman should have only one child in a year, and it has been so ever since.

from the *Myths of the Cherokee* by James Mooney

∼ END ∼

In this myth, an island called earth grows from mud floating on a sea. The animals send Buzzard to make the earth ready for them. When the earth is dry, the sun is set in place and the animals are given certain abilities. Men and women come to earth after this.

Trickster Tales

Trickster tales serve a variety of purposes in the Native American oral tradition. They are a source of entertainment; they often double as origin tales; and most importantly they express the values and beliefs of a specific culture.

Each trickster tale features a specific trickster character. Trickster characters, including Coyote, Raven, and "The Tricky One," encompass a kaleidoscope of human and nonhuman traits. The trickster characters can be difficult to define because they embody paradox; they are simultaneously sacred and profane, human and nonhuman, deceiving and deceived. The ultimate paradox of the trickster is that while seemingly lacking in morals, he is able to teach essential values of the culture through his actions.

"Coyote and the Another One" provides an example of the complexity and layering of meaning within a trickster tale.

PRIMARY SOURCE: TRICKSTER TALE

Coyote and the Another One

told by Charles Phillip Whitedog

Two Coyotes were crossing a farmer's field. Both Coyotes were strangers to each other. Just as they were about to introduce themselves they heard the Farmer yell, "There's a Coyote in the field!" The first Coyote turned and told the other to run!

Then they heard the Farmer yell, "And there goes another one!" Finally both Coyotes made it to the trees. "I never saw you before, I am Wanderer, I am a Coyote like you." The other Coyote said, "I am Sleek, but I am not a Coyote like you."

"Yes you are," said Wanderer.

"Oh no I am not," replied Sleek.

"Look, you have ears and a tail like mine, our fur and snout are

continued on page 22

Trickster Tales

PRIMARY SOURCE: TRICKSTER TALE   *continued from page 21*

the same. We are both Coyotes," Wanderer tried to explain. "Listen, let's run across the field."

Again the Farmer yelled, "There goes that darn Coyote. And there goes another one . . . again!"

When the Coyotes reached the other side of the field, Wanderer said, "There! Didn't you hear the Farmer? He called us both Coyotes."

Sleek said, "Yes I heard the Farmer. He called you a Coyote, but I am an 'Another One.'"

MORAL: Our problem is we are listening to the Farmer tell us who we are.

~ END ~

This tale can be interpreted on a variety of levels. It expresses the cultural value of knowing oneself and looking inside for a definition of oneself. Like many trickster tales, it uses the absence of such an act to emphasize its importance. The Another One, a trickster figure, does not know who he is and listens to an outside source (here, the farmer) to define him.

On another level, this tale can be read as an allegory for the Native Americans. It expresses the general threat of the white man (the farmer yelling at the coyotes), the danger of allowing the white man to define the Native American people, and the importance of solidarity among the Native Americans: "Look, you have ears and a tail like mine, our fur and snouts are the same. We are both Coyotes." By refusing to believe, the second coyote places both of them in harm's way a second time. The relationship between Native Americans and whites is a common theme in the trickster tradition.

Trickster tales have been around for centuries and continue to thrive. Throughout the ages trickster tales have made their mark on Native American culture and on many people outside the culture, illuminating ways to be in the world with other people and with nature.

Songs

Though entertainment was one purpose of Native American songs, music has been primarily a means of communicating with the supernatural. Songs were sung as prayers for rain or to cure the sick. They were performed before battles to bring success. A means of transmitting cultural heritage from generation to generation, types of songs ranged from ceremonial and healing songs received in dreams to war songs praying for a victory and a safe return home.

The repetition used in traditional songs serves as both a memory aid and a powerful and beautiful musical technique. When accompanied by drums and sometimes flutes, whistles, and dance, such songs are an integral part of ceremonial culture. The preservation of such songs is vital to recording accurately the rich oral tradition of Native Americans.

Many examples of written Native American literature are translations by American Romantics such as Henry Wadsworth Longfellow. These translations often reflect the white culture's notion of the "noble savage," and rely on Americanized language and literary form. While some have criticized Longfellow for failing to understand completely the native culture he portrayed in works such as Hiawatha, others have praised him for bringing to the American public one of their first views of the creative life of the Native American people.

~ **Notes**

PRIMARY SOURCE: SONG

The Song of the Lenape Warriors Going Against the Enemy
(Delaware)

O poor me!
Who am going out to fight the enemy,
And know not whether I shall return again,
To enjoy the embraces of my children
And my wife.
O poor creature!
Whose life is not in his own hands,
Who has no power over his own body,
But tries to do his duty
For the welfare of his nation.
O! thou Great Spirit above!
Take pity on my children
And on my wife!
Prevent their mourning on my account!
Grant that I may be successful in this attempt—
That I may slay my enemy,
And bring home the trophies of war
To my dear family and friends,
That we may rejoice together.

~ END ~

~ **Notes**

_____

_____

_____

_____

_____

_____

_____

_____

_____

_____

_____

First Encounters

When Christopher Columbus landed on a tiny Caribbean island in 1492, he called the inhabitants Indians because he thought he was near the East Indies in Asia. No one had tried the western route to India before, so Columbus and his crew were in uncharted lands. One of the first native men to try to communicate with Columbus inadvertently cut his hand on Columbus' sword. He didn't know what a sword was. Mistaken identity and injury thus symbolically marked the first recorded encounter between the native people of the Americas and the Europeans, who came west in increasing numbers over the next 500 years.

The first explorers' motivations for coming to the Americas were complex. Many came out of a desire for fame and adventure. Others came expecting to find great riches. European rulers had already sent explorers to India and China to bring back spices, silks, gold, jewelry, and other luxuries. Columbus, of course, was looking for a shortcut to these countries when he unexpectedly bumped into a new world. Once the European monarchs realized that Columbus had

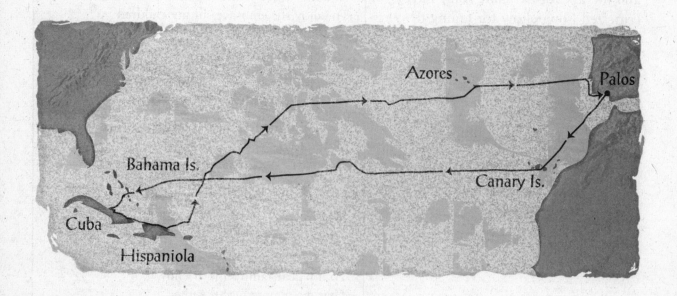

led the way to two previously unknown continents, they put their best explorers to work finding out what wealth they could gain from these new lands.

Not all motivations for coming to the Americas were overtly economic ones. Reports of the existence of people in the Americas stirred many people to come to spread Christianity. Others, such as the English Puritans, came seeking the religious freedom that they were denied in their homeland. Even though they endured persecution, both Catholics and Protestants believed Christianity to be the only true religion. Nonbelievers were considered enemies of God and had to be converted by persuasion or force.

The story of cultural contact, like the story of America itself, would not be complete without the experiences of the Africans who were brought here as slaves. European slave trade began in the 1400s when the Portuguese started enslaving Africans. That is why enslaved Africans accompanied most of the Spanish and Portuguese explorers to the Americas. In fact, it was recorded that one of the three men who survived with Cabeza de Vaca on his disastrous journey was an enslaved African named Estéban.

Africans were first brought in large numbers to the West Indies to provide labor for the vast sugar plantations and silver mines. At first, the Spanish plantation owners tried to use Indian labor, but the native peoples proved too susceptible to European diseases and were unable to withstand the harsh treatment of their masters. Africans took the native people's place. Before long, English colonists were also participating in the slave trade. In 1619, twelve years after the founding of the first permanent English settlement in the Americas at Jamestown, Virginia, 20 Africans were brought there as indentured servants. Eighteen years later, the first American-built slave ship, the *Desire*, set sail from Marblehead, Massachusetts. Thousands of Africans would be robbed of their freedom while the English colonies thrived off the forced African labor.

~ **Notes**

_____
_____
_____
_____
_____
_____
_____
_____
_____
_____
_____
_____
_____
_____
_____
_____
_____
_____

Exploration and Its Effects

In the 1500s, the Age of Discovery was marked by European exploration. Actually, exploration began before that time with the Portuguese and Spanish. Europeans took to the sea after the land route to the East was cut off due to wars with the Turks. They needed to find a way to reach the sources of spices, silks, and other luxuries that the East had to offer.

The Portuguese explorers initially were seeking new trade routes, but ultimately colonized Brazil. Eventually, the desire to acquire land and riches became the primary motive for exploration. Spanish and British explorers set out with the intention of conquering and colonizing new lands.

Instead of encountering empty lands, the European explorers came upon native civilizations nearly everywhere they went. Their initial attempts to befriend the indigenous people did not last long; soon the European explorers turned to exploiting the people and obliterating their cultures.

Many examples exist of the destruction of native culture as the result of European arrivals. Columbus' arrival on Hispaniola in 1492 brought disease and hardship to the Taino Indians of that island, leading to the extinction of their entire population in little more than 50 years. The Taino and other Caribbean people on neighboring islands survived although their populations also felt the impact of the European conquerors. While the exact population of Arawak in the islands at the time of Columbus' arrival is uncertain, with estimates ranging from a few hundred thousand up to eight million, it is generally believed that their numbers had been reduced to 600 by 1531. Even more lives—about 23 million—were lost as Hernando Cortés overtook the Aztec empire and Francesco Pizarro conquered the Inca of Peru. All of this was done for the purpose of gaining wealth and power for Spain. Many of the remaining natives were forced into labor or contracted viruses for which they had no immunity.

The same fate lay ahead for the Native Americans of North America. The British set up colonies in territory previously inhabited by indigenous cultures. Attempts were made to maintain friendly relations between the colonists and natives, but there were too many cultural differences. The British were often intolerant of religions other than Christianity and sometimes viewed such unbelievers as heathens worthy only of slavery.

Native Americans were displaced from their homes, their lands were destroyed, and they were exposed to devastating diseases. Much of their time was now spent trading or warring with the colonists. Bereft of their former autonomy, native populations were eventually wiped out as a result of the European arrival.

Another effect of the establishment of colonies was the plantation system. In North and South America, as well as the Caribbean, plantations sprang up growing sugar cane, cotton, and tobacco. These money-making industries led to the need for manual labor. Some poor Englishmen would pledge several years of work in payment for passage to the New World. Eventually they would earn their freedom.

Seeking more free labor, Europeans attempted to enslave native peoples, forcing them to work on plantations. The Spanish set up the *encomienda* system to establish native slavery. In this system, the natives were forced to pay tribute for use of the land. Much of the time, Native Americans were taken from their homes and forced to labor as payment. But Native Americans knew the territory so well that they were often able to escape. Without native help, the Europeans turned to Africa as a source of workers, and so began the importation of enslaved Africans.

What the Portuguese had begun in 1441 with the slave trade eventually grew into millions of Africans living as slaves in the Americas. European exploration created an entirely new culture, based on racism and oppression, and the institution of slavery thrived for hundreds of years to come.

∽ **Notes**

_____

_____

_____

_____

_____

_____

_____

_____

_____

_____

_____

_____

_____

_____

_____

_____

_____

_____

_____

_____

_____

Earliest American Literature and African American Literature

The earliest American literature was practical in nature and included diaries, journals, letters, histories and reports. Fictional writing did not appear until the struggle to survive in the new land had given way to a more routine existence for the colonists. This section will compare the literature of exploration and histories and reports. We will also look at the origins of African American literature, another important component in our literary history.

Literature of Exploration

With the explosion of exploration came a comparable explosion in the literature of exploration. Explorers began recording and publishing their adventures and encounters. From this time period comes Christopher Columbus' *Journal*, Cabeza de Vaca's *La Relación*, and Marco Polo's *The Travels of Marco Polo*, each centering around the common themes of adventure, travel, hardships, and encounters with natives of various countries.

These exploration texts also share a general European ethnocentricity in their views of native cultures. The indigenous peoples are seen as savages, uncivilized and ignorant. For example, in *La Relación*, Cabeza de Vaca refers to them as "wild, untaught savages howling like brutes." Columbus comments in his *Journal*, "They ought to make good and skilled servants." He also makes the assumption that they have no religion. These attitudes, in the end, turned out to be deadly for the native populations, who suffered brutal treatment at the hands of the explorers and conquerors.

Histories and Reports

Shortly after the rise of exploration literature, another form of literature became popular. People began to write histories and records of the colonies, as well as

Copyright © McDougal Littell Inc.

descriptions of everyday life. Much of the literature served the purpose of reporting back to the kings and queens of the imperial countries, giving updates on the state of affairs in the colonies. Such writings include Thomas Harriot's *A Briefe and True Report of the New-Found Land of Virginia*, Captain John Smith's *The General History of Virginia, New England, and the Summer Isles*, and William Bradford's *Of Plymouth Plantation*.

Like the literature of exploration, these accounts often recorded relationships with the native peoples. Harriot, for example, dedicates an entire section of his *Report* to the Native Americans. He titles it "Concerning the Nature and Manners of the People." Captain John Smith provides highly romanticized tales of his capture by the Native Americans and his experiences with Pocahontas. And William Bradford chronicles the daily struggle of the Puritans' existence and their relationship with the Native Americans they encounter.

∼ **Notes**
Use a Venn diagram to compare and contrast the literature of exploration with histories and reports.

Literature of Exploration

Similarities of Exploration and Histories & Reports

Histories and Reports

PRIMARY SOURCE: JOURNAL

from *Bradford's History of Plymouth Plantation, 1606-1646*

by William Bradford

All this while the Indians came skulking about them, and would sometimes show them selves aloofe of, but when any aproached near them, they would rune away. And once they stoale away their tools wher they had been at worke, and were gone to diner. But about the 16. of March a certaine Indian came bouldly amongst them, and spoke to them in broken English, Which they could well understand, but marvelled at it. At length they understood by discourse with him, that he was not of these parts, but belonged to the eastrene parts, wher some English-ships came to fhish, with whom he was aquainted, and could name sundrie of them by their names, amongst whom he had gott his

continued on page 30

language. He became proftable to them in aquainting them with many things concerning the state of the country in the east-parts wher he lived, which was afterwards profitable unto them . . . His name was Samaset; he tould them also of another Indian whos name was Squanto, a native of this place, who had been in England and could speake better English then him selfe. Being, after some time of entertainmente and gifts, dismist, a while after he came againe, and 5. more with him, and they brought againe all the tooles that were stolen away before, and made way for the coming of their great Sachem, called Massasoyt . . . [T]hey made a peace with him . . . in these terms.

1. That neither he nor any of his, should injurie or doe hurte to any of their peopl.

2. That if any of his did any hurte to any of theirs, he should send the offender, that they might punish him.

3. That if any thing were taken away from any of theirs, he should cause it to be restored; and they should doe the like to his.

4. If any did unjustly warr against him, they would aide him; if any warr against them, he should aide them.

5. He should send to his neighbours confederats, to certifie them of this, that they might not wrong them, but might be likewise comprised in the conditions of peace.

6. That when ther men came to them, they should leave their bows and arrows behind them. . . .

They begane now to gather in the small harvest they had, and to fitte up their houses and dwellings against winter, being all well recovered in health and strenght, and had all things in good plenty; for as some were thus imployed in affairs abroad, others were excersised in fishing, aboute codd, and bass, and other fish, of which they tooke good store,

continued on page 31

of which every family had their portion. All the sommer ther was no wante. And now begane to come in store of foule, as winter aproached, of which this place did abound. . . . And besides water foule, ther was great store of wild Turkies, of which they tooke many, besids venison, etc. . . .

Yet at length it begane to languish sore, and some of the drier grounds were partched like withered hay, part whereof was never recovered. Upon which they sett a parte a solemne day of humilliation, to seek the Lord by humble and fervente prayer, in this great distrese. And he was pleased to give them a gracious and speedy answer, both to thier owne and the Indeans admiration, that lived amongest them. [T]oward evening it begane to overcast, and shortly after to raine, with shuch sweete and gentle showers, as gave them cause of rejoyceing, and blesing God. It came, without either wind, or thunder, or any violence, and by degreese in that abundance, as that the earth was thorowly wete and soked therwith. Which did so apparently revive and quicken the decayed corne and other fruits, as was wonderfull to see, and made the Indeans astonished to behold; and afterwards the Lord sent them shuch seasonable showers, with enterchange of faire warme weather, as, through his blessing, caused a fruitfull and liberall harvest, to their no small comforte and rejoycing. For which mercie (in time conveniente) they also sett aparte a day of thanksgiveing. . . .

∽ END ∾

Though such accounts as these also contain elements of ethnocentricity, the focus seems to be more on the relationships established between the Native Americans and the colonists than on an evaluation of the peoples' lives, beliefs, and physical characteristics. Letters and journals provide a valuable glimpse into the past, but the whole story may be harder to discover.

∽ **Notes**

African American Literature

It is not surprising that with the establishment of the institution of slavery in the colonies, there came the growth of a black literary tradition in what would later become America. Naturally, the people who were imported as slaves from various parts of Africa brought their oral traditions with them. These oral traditions then mixed with the cultural influence of the colonists, including the influences of Christianity. The experiences in this new land provoked the Africans to deal with the themes of hardship and escape in the tales and songs of the enslaved people.

The plantation owners would often not allow the Africans to participate in their oral traditions that included drumming and singing, so the people came up with new ways to express themselves. Eventually, from the institution of slavery, came spirituals such as "Go Down, Moses" and "Swing Low, Sweet Chariot." Also, from that tradition came the trickster tales of Brer Rabbit and Uncle Remus. These songs and tales provided a means to express cultural beliefs and values, as well as exchange information. Many examples also provided a message of hope of a freedom soon to come.

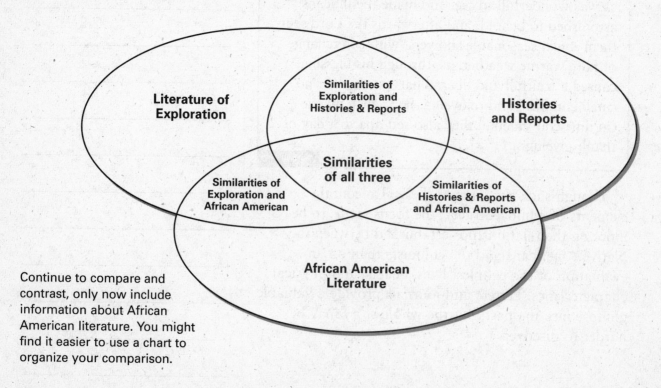

Continue to compare and contrast, only now include information about African American literature. You might find it easier to use a chart to organize your comparison.

The Origin of Colonial Government

On the voyage to the New World, the pilgrims wrote the Mayflower Compact, as a preventative measure against disruption in the new colony. Some of the people were "not well affected to unity and concord," noted Governor William Bradford; the Compact established a form of government with authority.

Half of the passengers aboard the Mayflower did not survive the first winter; the rest endured, their traditions becoming the foundation of America.

PRIMARY SOURCE: GOVERNMENT DOCUMENT

Mayflower Compact 1620

IN THE NAME OF GOD, AMEN. We, whose names are underwritten, the Loyal Subjects of our dread Sovereign Lord King James, by the Grace of God, of Great Britain, France, and Ireland, King, Defender of the Faith, &c. Having undertaken for the Glory of God, and Advancement of the Christian Faith, and the Honour of our King and Country, a Voyage to plant the first Colony in the northern Parts of Virginia; Do by these Presents, solemnly and mutually, in the Presence of God and one another, covenant and combine ourselves together into a civil Body Politick, for our better Ordering and Preservation, and Furtherance of the Ends aforesaid: And by Virtue hereof do enact, constitute, and frame, such just and equal Laws, Ordinances, Acts, Constitutions, and Officers, from time to time, as shall be thought most meet and convenient for the general Good of the Colony; unto which we promise all due Submission and Obedience. IN WITNESS whereof we have hereunto subscribed our names at Cape-Cod the eleventh of November, in the Reign of our Sovereign Lord King James, of England, France, and Ireland, the eighteenth, and of Scotland the fifty-fourth, Anno Domini; 1620.

 END

~ Notes

From Colony to Country

EVENTS IN AMERICAN LITERATURE

1620 **1700**

1624 Captain John Smith writes *General History in Virginia*

1640 *Bay Psalm Book* is first book printed in America

1666 Anne Bradstreet, first notable colonial poet, writes "Upon the Burning of Our House"

1678 Bradstreet publishes "To My Dear and Loving Husband," not originally intended for "public view"

1682 Mary Rowlandson's captivity narrative is published

1683(?) *The New England Primer* is published

1704 *Boston Newsletter*, first American newspaper is established; John Williams is captured by Native Americans and French Canadians. He writes a bestselling memoir

1732 Benjamin Franklin initiates a circulating library in Philadelphia; Franklin's *Poor Richard's Almanack* is published

1741 Jonathan Edwards delivers sermon, "Sinners in the Hands of an Angry God"

EVENTS IN NORTH AMERICA

1620 **1700**

1630 About 1,000 Puritans establish Massachusetts Bay Colony

1676 Puritans' victory in King Philip's War ends Native American resistance in New England colonies

1682 Quakers led by William Penn begin living in peace with Native Americans in Pennsylvania (to c. 1752)

1688 Quakers voice opposition to slavery

1691 New charter provides for religious tolerance in Massachusetts, weakening Puritans' control

1692 Witchcraft trials take place in Salem, Massachusetts

1763 British defeat French in French and Indian War, and claim land east of Mississippi River, including Canada

1765 British Parliament passes Stamp Act, which levies tax on colonies to help pay off British debts

EVENTS IN THE WORLD

1620 **1700**

1632 Indian emperor Shah Jahan builds Taj Mahal, over the next 22 years

1643 Louis XIV begins 72-year reign in France

1649 Oliver Cromwell and Puritans execute King Charles I of England

1687 Sir Isaac Newton presents law of gravity

1721 Edo (Tokyo) in Japan becomes world's largest city

1748 French philosopher Baron de Montesquieu publishes *Spirit of the Laws*

1780

1773 Phillis Wheatley's *Poems on Various Subjects, Religious and Moral* is the first book of poetry published by an African American

1775 In speech to the Second Virginia Convention, Patrick Henry makes plea for armed resistance against British

1776 Thomas Paine publishes *Common Sense*; Declaration of Independence is written by Thomas Jefferson

1782 Michel-Guillaume Jean de Crèvecoeur publishes *Letters from an American Farmer*, a collection of 12 essays on life in America

1789 *The Interesting Narrative of the Life of Olaudah Equiano* is published

1780

1773 To protest new British tax on tea, enraged colonists stage Boston Tea Party, dumping huge amounts of tea into Boston Harbor

1775 "Shot heard round the world" is fired on Lexington Green in Massachusetts, starting Revolutionary War

1780 Esther De Berdt Reed helps raise $300,000 to help clothe the desperate Continental Army

1781 British surrender to General George Washington at Yorktown, ending Revolutionary War

1789 George Washington is elected first president of United States (to 1797)

1791 Bill of Rights becomes part of U.S. Constitution

1793 Eli Whitney invents cotton gin

1796 Washington declines to run for third term and establishes presidential succession

1780

1762 Catherine the Great begins rule of Russia (to 1796)

1776 Adam Smith publishes *The Wealth of Nations*

1789 French Revolution begins (to 1794)

1793 French King Louis XVI is executed by guillotine

1795 Poland disappears from map of Europe after last partition

∾ Notes

Use a cluster diagram to take notes that will help you analyze the different aspects of Puritan life that were important to the early colonists.

Puritan Life

_____

_____

_____

_____

_____

_____

_____

_____

_____

_____

_____

Between Heaven and Hell

The colonists of the first settlement in Jamestown, Virginia, were religious people. However, religion did not dominate the culture of Virginia as it did the culture of the Puritans who came to the New World and settled in New England. According to the American writer and humorist H. L. Mencken, a Puritan is one who suspects that "somewhere someone is having a good time." The enduring image of life in colonial Virginia, by contrast, is that of a monied landowner who almost always was enjoying himself.

Both of these images are based upon a generalization of traits that were found in reality. The term "Puritan," for instance, came from their emphasis on "purity" in their mode of reading the Bible directly, with a minimum of mediation and interpretation. Their intention in the New World was to be an example to others in their commitment to a life based on religious principles. "The eyes of all people are on us," proclaimed John Winthrop, the first governor of the Massachusetts Bay Colony. Winthrop's conviction of the world-historical centrality of the experience of his small band of believers became a key element of American national character.

The first religious people to settle in New England were, however, not the Puritans, but the Pilgrims. The Pilgrims were separatists. Although they shared the same theology as the Puritans, they believed that the Church of England could not be reformed so they went to the New World. For the Pilgrims, every experience was a direct message from God. They saw their early harsh years as a challenge from God, a test of their faith. Naturally, they saw their first good harvest (with help from the Native Americans) as a reward from God.

Both the Pilgrims and the Puritans viewed everything through the lens of a deeper spiritual meaning. They felt that material wealth was what God intended. Since all of life related to the will of God, hard work would lead to a heavenly reward. Puritans put great stock into

Notes

education and were the first in the colonies to establish a printing press, free public grammar schools, and a college (Harvard). The entire community supported the college, down to poor farmers who donated wheat to ensure its economic survival. Puritan leaders wanted to educate lay people as well as ministers. In creating a venue for teaching their children about their religion, they also created a vehicle for independent thought. By the mid-1600s, there were as many university graduates in New England as there were in the mother country.

The literature of the Puritans is a religiously informed literature, rich and filled with life. Of course, much Puritan writing was composed of sermons and nonfiction that focused on self-examination and faith in God. And while it may not be "entertaining" in the way in which we define the word today, Puritan religious histories, sermons, and narratives were intellectually stimulating and exciting to their audience. A sermon, that most religious piece of Puritan literature, could easily last an hour. Melodramatic contrasts between good and evil, logical exposition, and powerful conclusions made a forcible impact. Despite their theology and their image as pleasure-hating prudes, the Puritans' view of their lives was far from dour. Attention to religious concepts filled their hearts with joy. They danced and sang religious songs, played games, and held celebrations with large feasts. The Puritans of the Massachusetts Bay Colony were even known to drink beer and other alcoholic beverages on occasion. They did tend to look down on certain activities such as playing cards; not because they considered them evil, but because they saw them as a waste of valuable time.

A Puritan minister, Richard Rogers, told his followers to enjoy sports such as hunting and swimming in order to "refresh" themselves—giving thanks for the luxury of free time. He encouraged people to blend an equal amount of work, relaxation, and sleep in a 24-hour day. On Sunday, Puritans were admonished to play games, visit, or read. The idea was not to prescribe what people did on Sunday but to free them from work for one day each week.

~ **Notes**

Although they wore black on Sundays—which fits the image we have of them—on other days the Puritans' clothing was bright and colorful. They used their clothing to express themselves, and the fine material displayed their prosperity to their peers. They also had a strong sense of visual beauty, which can be seen in the architecture of the period, and in shipbuilding and other crafts and trades.

While women were subservient to men in the religious arena, they were expected to understand household finances and legal matters. They were also valued as partners. William Gouge, a Puritan preacher, urged married couples to be cheerful and giving. Marriage, along with the physical relationship between husband and wife, was seen as a gift from God. Families were cherished, and children were not always just small adults, an often-heard criticism of the Puritans' child-rearing beliefs.

On the other hand, the Puritans *were* inflexible in their religious faith and intolerant of viewpoints different from their own, even among their own ranks. A notable case is that of Anne Hutchinson (1591–1643). Winthrop described her in his journal as "a woman of ready wit and bold spirit, [who] brought over with her two dangerous errors: 1. That the person of the Holy Ghost dwells in a justified person. 2. That no sanctification can help to evidence to us our justification. . . ." Having her own ideas, and, worse, sharing them with others, resulted in Hutchinson's banishment. Fear of dissent, regardless of its merits, would ultimately lead to the excesses of the Salem Witch Trials (see p. 43).

During the 1600s Puritanism reached its fullest and perhaps purest development. But living in a new territory among unfriendly Native Americans and French Canadians was dangerous physically: living with spiritual rigidity closed more doors than it opened. Eventually, with the coming of the Great Awakening, the first settlers had to adapt to, and embrace, new ideas.

The Captivity Narrative

All literature of the Puritan era was informed by these particular beliefs: Human beings were thought to be essentially evil, having inherited original sin; they had limited control over their destiny; and the Bible was the only guide needed for all behavior on Earth.

Just as their daily lives fell within a religious context, so did their relationships with Native Americans. Initially, the Pilgrims were able to befriend Native Americans, but conflicts, especially over land ownership, eventually arose between Native Americans and new settlers. The immigrants felt entitled to claim the land for themselves, while Native Americans believed that the land "belonged" to no one. English settlers also made little effort to introduce their religion to many Native Americans, so the two groups had little in common.

Between 1677 and 1750, during wars between the settlers and the Native Americans, the Native Americans captured over 1,500 settlers. Sometimes Native Americans sought captives to use as hostages to exchange for money. They also took captives to replace family members who had died during hostilities with settlers. Inevitably, Native Americans also became players in the religious struggle between the Catholic French Canadians and English Puritans. Native Americans and French Canadians sometimes partnered in attacks against the Puritans, although their aims differed. Eventually, a fair number of captives were released—after months or years and prolonged negotiations.

A surprising number of such captives wrote and published accounts of their plight. These texts, called "captivity narratives," were widely read as stories of enduring ordeals that promised salvation, much like the Puritans' daily lives. The narratives also reinforced the Puritans' need to feel superior to Native Americans. One of the most famous captivity narratives was that of Mary Rowlandson. She was

_____

_____

_____

_____

_____

_____

_____

_____

_____

_____

_____

_____

_____

_____

_____

_____

_____

captured in a raid in Lancaster, Massachusetts, in 1676 along with 23 others, and was held for almost three months. Eventually, she was released in exchange for £20. While in captivity she traveled with her captors through Massachusetts, New Hampshire, and Connecticut. Her narrative, excerpted below, was published in 1682. It stood out then, as it does now, for its detail and passion.

PRIMARY SOURCE: CAPTIVITY NARRATIVE

from *A True History of the Captivity and Restoration of Mrs. Mary Rowlandson*
by Mary Rowlandson

. . . I must turn my back upon the town, and travel with them into the vast and desolate wilderness, I knew not whither. It is not my tongue, or pen, can express the sorrows of my heart, and bitterness of my spirit that I had at this departure: but God was with me in a wonderful manner, carrying me along, and bearing up my spirit, that it did not quite fail. One of the Indians carried my poor wounded babe upon a horse; it went moaning all along, "I shall die, I shall die." I went on foot after it, with sorrow that cannot be expressed. At length I took it off the horse, and carried it in my arms till my strength failed, and I fell down with it. Then they set me upon a horse with my wounded child in my lap, and there being no furniture upon the horse's back, as we were going down a steep hill we both fell over the horse's head, at which they, like inhumane creatures, laughed, and rejoiced to see it, though I thought we should there have ended our days, as overcome with so many difficulties. But the Lord renewed my strength still, and carried me along, that I might see more of His power; yea, so much that I could never have thought of, had I not experienced it, . . .

When I lived in prosperity, having the comforts of the world about me, my relations by me, my

continued on page 41

PRIMARY SOURCE: CAPTIVITY NARRATIVE *cont'd from page 40*

heart cheerful, and taking little care for anything, and yet seeing many, whom I preferred before myself, under many trials and afflictions, in sickness, weakness, poverty, losses, crosses, and cares of the world, I should be sometimes jealous. . . . But now I see the Lord had His time to scourge and chasten me. . . . When God calls a person to anything, and through never so many difficulties, yet He is fully able to carry them through and make them see, and say they have been gainers thereby. And I hope I can say in some measure, as David did, "It is good for me that I have been afflicted." . . . I have learned to look beyond present and smaller troubles, and to be quieted under them.

∽ END ∽

Notes

Throughout her narrative, the Puritan view of God is ever-present. Rowlandson rationalizes all horrific events as caused by God's wrath, levied on deserving sinners by a divine Father who is anxious to purge them of sin. Similarly, she rationalizes positive circumstances as being blessed by God's mercy. The captivity is a test to be endured. The bondage is a metaphor for the bondage of the human spirit, which can only be freed by God's arbitrary grace. The captivity is also an exile—the literal exile of the Puritans' separation from England and the spiritual exile of all humans who have not accepted God into their hearts.

The Puritan view of Native Americans as savage beasts is evident in all captivity narratives, which generally begin with a slaughter of white people, followed by a litany of hardships suffered at the hands of Native Americans. While these were horrifying events, there is no sense of perspective that the raids were part of mutual hostilities that had gone on for years. There is also no mention of any prior aggression on the part of settlers. Finally, the narratives include few references to decent acts by Native Americans, although they happened and were documented by others.

_____

_____

_____

_____

_____

_____

_____

Next to Mary Rowlandson, John Williams's captivity narrative is the best known. He was captured in Deerfield, Massachusetts, in February 1704, in a night raid by almost three hundred Native Americans and French Canadians. Williams was a prominent member of the New England clergy and his Canadian captors wanted him as a hostage to get one of their prisoners released. The Native Americans forced over one hundred prisoners to march to Canada. Many, including Williams's wife, did not survive the 300-mile march north. Williams, and others with him, were held for two years. His memoir, *The Redeemed Captive Returning to Zion,* became a bestseller. To him, Native Americans were another way God was testing Puritans. Like Rowlandson, Williams considered God's anger at his flock as just, and thought his mercy warm and welcome. But while Rowlandson's struggle was more physical and emotional, Williams's was more spiritual. The key distinguishing element in Williams's narrative was his concern that his Canadian captors were trying to convert him to Catholicism. Ironically, Williams's daughter ended up converting to Roman Catholicism and marrying a member of the Mohawk people.

PRIMARY SOURCE: MEMOIR

from *The Redeemed Captive Returning to Zion*
by John Williams

My Master took hold of my hand to force me to *Cross my self,* but I struggled with him, and would not suffer him to guide my hand; upon this he pulled off a *Crucifix* from his own neck, and bad me *Kiss* it; but I refused once and again; he told *me he would dash out my brains with his Hatchet if I refused.* I told him I should sooner choose death than to Sin against God; then he ran and catched up his Hatchet, and acted as tho' he would have dashed out my Brains; seeing I was not moved, he threw down his Hatchet, *saying he would first bite off all my nails if I still refused;* I gave him my hand and told him, I was ready to suffer, he set his teeth in my thumbnails and gave a gripe with his teeth, and then said, *no good Minister, no love God, as bad as the Devil;* and so left off. I have reason to bless God who strengthened me to withstand; by this he was so discouraged as never more to meddle with me about my Religion.

∽ END ∽

The Puritan Backlash

The Salem Witch Trials

Perhaps it is inevitable that a society as closely controlled as that of the Puritans would lead to extremes. As their ministers warned of hell and damnation, they also told of the intrigue of the devil. Like many other New England colonies in the late 1600s, Salem found itself in a transition from an agricultural, communal culture to a secular, commercial society with less religious influence. In addition, there had been an outbreak of smallpox, and King Charles II had revoked the charter of the Massachusetts Bay Colony, cutting the settlers off from their homeland. Finally, there was constant anxiety about Native American and French Canadian attacks. Subjected to such stresses, Puritans allowed their fear to mount and feed on itself.

In the winter of 1692, a small group of teenage girls were listening to exciting tales of magic and playing fortune-telling games with Tituba, a slave from the West Indies. Such games were strictly forbidden, so the girls may have felt guilty. Perhaps fearful that others would find them out, the girls accused Tituba of casting spells on them. They fell into babbling fits and extended their accusations to other women in Salem.

The accusation of witchcraft was not in itself so alarming. People in both America and Europe believed in witchery. What was surprising was the infectious nature of the accusations. Witnesses and accusers spoke of visions and visitations from spirits that could hardly be objectively examined. In the presence of an unseen and imaginary threat, almost everyone was potentially under suspicion. Those who were accused of witchcraft often became accusers, blaming others for their passionate fits.

By the following autumn, more than 20 people had been executed. By the end of 1692, around 200 people had been imprisoned. When some began to question the trials, the hysteria waned. Some of the accused clearly were not witches, and ministers and judges knew that wrongful executions had taken place. Increase Mather went so far as to state that it would be better to allow

Notes

Take notes on the selection using a cause and effect diagram to help you examine why the Puritans might have been vulnerable to the hysterical environment of the Salem Witch Trials.

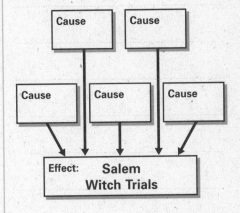

_____

_____

_____

_____

_____

_____

_____

_____

_____

_____

those who were suspected of being witches to go free than to unjustly punish innocent people. Cotton Mather spoke out against the use of "spectral evidence"—testimony based on contact with spirits. Finally, the governor ended the court sessions, and the accused who had survived the ritual were finally released.

PRIMARY SOURCE: LEGAL TRANSCRIPT

Examination of Mary Warren, April 19, 1692

Mary Warren, You stand here charged with sundry acts of Witchcraft, what do you say for your selfe, are you guilty, or not?

[Mary]   I am inocent. . . .

. . . Now Mary Warren fell into a fit, & some of the afflicted cryed out that she was going to confess, but Goody Korey, & Procter, & his wife came in, in their apparition, & struck her down, & said she should tell nothing.

Mary Warren continued a good space in a fit, that she did neither see, nor hear, nor speak.

Afterwards she started up, & said I will speak & cryed out, Oh! I am sorry for it, I am sorry for it, & wringed her hands, & fell a little while into a fit again & then came to speak, but immediately her Teeth were set, & then she fell into a violent fit, & cryed out, Oh Lord help me, Oh good Lord save me!

And then afterwards cryed again, I will tell, I will tell, & then fell into a dead fit againe. . . .

Have you signed the Devils book?

[Mary] No.

Have you not touch it?

[Mary]   No.

Then she fell into fits againe, & was sent forth for air. . . .

From *The Salem Witchcraft Papers: Verbatim Transcripts of the Legal Documents of the Salem Witchcraft Outbreak of 1692*

~ END ~

The after-effects of the trials were numerous. Homes and fields had been abandoned during the trials. For several years afterward, people had to contend with bad crop yields. The Puritans felt that God was punishing them for accusing others unjustly. They declared a fasting and prayer day to ask forgiveness, and a new, more personal, church was founded.

The Great Awakening

Although it occurred almost forty years later, the Great Awakening was a by-product of the reevaluation that took place after the Salem Witch Trials. The Great Awakening refers to a series of religious revivals that were stimulated by a wide-felt need for renewed dedication to religious convictions.

In the mid-1700s, England, Wales, Scotland, and Germany were energized by renewed religious interest. In the United States, this revival of religious fervor also fed on societal conflicts between older, more religious settlers and recent, less religious immigrants, as well as between rural farmers and more urban businessmen. Also, conflict arose between older Puritans who worried about the youth being frivolous and the growing number of children born out of wedlock.

Jonathan Edwards is considered to have been the most significant preacher during this period. Edwards was one of the last preachers in the traditional Puritan mold. He defended old-style Calvinist rigidity against what he perceived as wanton liberalism.

In his sermons, Edwards was able effectively to combine religion with other current intellectual movements. He wove into his texts Isaac Newton's physics discoveries and the philosophical arguments of John Locke. His sermons were logical arguments for accepting God, and his delivery was quiet and contemplative. His most familiar work, "Sinners in the Hands of an Angry God," painted a clear picture of the divine power of God, the low position of humans, and the inevitability of hell for sinners.

Notes

_____

_____

_____

_____

_____

_____

_____

_____

_____

_____

_____

_____

_____

_____

_____

_____

_____

While initially effective, Edwards's sermons eventually lost their impact. People became alienated from his harsh message. In addition, Americans were moving toward a more forgiving faith that emphasized personal responsibility for one's moral behavior. Edwards was eventually relieved of his post at Northampton because of his overbearing, strict attitude. His dismissal signaled a rejection of the old Puritan life, or the "New England Way." His works continued to inspire debate, however, about free will and destiny.

As a result of the Great Awakening, Christianity flourished in the colonies, although established religious institutions lost some of their power. Believers began to rely on their personal experience of God to reinforce their faith, as opposed to blindly obeying church doctrine. Baptists and Methodists emerged as important new groups. The Great Awakening also reached out to groups that had been marginalized by traditional practice. Frontier groups, women, and African Americans were attracted to religion as never before. The established social classes were challenged—a development that undermined the plan of religion as the theological rationale for social hierarchies.

The new democracy and tolerance in religion was a precursor to an impending political and social movement—the American Revolution. As tensions escalated between the colonies and England, religious energies became focused on the need to establish a new and independent society.

The Right To Be Free

Revolutionary Voices

"No taxation without representation!" "Give me liberty, or give me death!" "We hold these truths to be self-evident. . . ." "We the people. . . ." Many famous phrases have come from the American Revolution. Behind the rhetoric lie major philosophical ideas that transformed thirteen British colonies into a nation and laid the groundwork for democratic institutions worldwide.

On the surface, the conflict between England and its American colonies was about money—specifically, unfair taxation. On a deeper level, what gave the rebellious colonists the mental strength needed for something as dangerous as revolution came essentially from two sources: the Bible and the writings of English philosopher John Locke.

Central to Locke's theory was the notion of "natural rights." In addition to life and liberty, the right to own property was considered a natural right. If any government abridged that right—by levying taxes without the consent of the property owners, for example—then the people could organize a new government. The spirit of Locke is reflected in Jefferson's eloquent opening to the Declaration of Independence. Locke's ideas of property rights were also echoed in the wording of the U.S. Constitution.

During the Revolution, many preachers recounted Bible stories of unjust rulers who burdened the people with high taxes and unjust laws. In Patrick Henry's famous words, "Give me liberty, or give me death," one can hear numerous references to God and the Bible.

The Spirit of the Revolution: Abigail Adams

The Revolutionary state of mind was embodied in many individuals—men *and* women. One of those who personified this spirit was Abigail Adams, wife of the second president, John Adams. She combined social and political curiosity with a strong sense of duty.

The Gadsden flag, created in 1776, is believed to be the first flag of the U.S. Navy; variations of the design were adopted by some minutemen militias.

Benjamin Franklin provided this interpretation of the rattlesnake in a letter to the Pennsylvania Journal *in 1775:*

[The Rattle-Snake] never begins an attack, nor, when once engaged, ever surrenders. . . I counted [the rattles] and found them just thirteen, exactly the number of Colonies . . . [H]ow firmly they are united together, so as never to be separated . . . One of those rattles singly is incapable of producing sound, but . . . thirteen together, is sufficient to alarm the boldest man living.

Join Or Die, *by Ben Franklin, warned the colonies to unite against the enemy in the French and Indian War. It appeared in the Pennsylvania Gazette in 1754.*

_____

_____

_____

_____

Abigail Adams was an articulate woman with opinions and insights she readily shared with her husband, John Adams, such as those in her famous letter of March 31, 1776:

. . . remember the ladies, and be more generous and favorable to them than your ancestors. Do not put such unlimited power into the hands of the husbands. . . . If particular care and attention is not paid to the ladies, we are determined to foment a rebellion, and will not hold ourselves bound by any laws in which we have no voice or representation.

The volumes of letters she left behind serve as a literary pathway through a formative time in the history of the United States.

Abigail read widely during childhood, although she was later embarrassed that her lack of formal education was betrayed by the poor punctuation and spelling in her letters. She met John Adams when she was 15 years old, and he 27. Their relationship developed into a strong intellectual and romantic bond. Living in Massachusetts, the couple sympathized with the growing discontent in the colonies. When John was elected to serve in the first Continental Congress, Abigail respected his call, even though it meant she had to run their farm as well as care for their children. She managed the staff, supervised the planting, oversaw the purchase and care of livestock, and handled all of the budgeting.

Abigail kept in touch with her husband through constant correspondence. Increasingly her letter-writing expands from personal matters to those of national importance. Abigail was smart, opinionated, and insightful. She also wrote to other political figures, including Jefferson.

Abigail felt strongly that a woman's role was as important as a man's. She supported education and legal and political rights for women, even if those rights would be exercised at home rather than in the public eye. Her concern for women's education was unusual for her time. Most women's goals were limited to getting married and raising a family. Abigail thought that both men and women were like "planets," and that each should "shine in their own orbit." She felt that because women were responsible for the education of young children, they should be adequately trained for the task.

In 1776, she wrote to Adams to remind him of the need to include women in the nation's goals of independence. In a letter often referred to as "Remember the Ladies," she asked that the new nation's founding fathers give women a "voice, or Representation." She was one of the first American women to raise this issue.

As her husband ascended in politics, first to the vice presidency under George Washington and then to the presidency, Abigail worked closely with him as partner and adviser. Although she promoted some unpopular views—such as her open hostility to France, her disagreements with Jefferson, and her support of the Alien and Sedition Acts—she mellowed once her husband left office. Abigail encouraged Adams to renew his relationship with Jefferson, which lasted until both men died on July 4, 1826—the fiftieth anniversary of the signing of the Declaration of Independence. Seven years after Abigail's death in 1818, her son, John Quincy Adams, became the nation's sixth president. Now Abigail Adams evoked the energy, determination, and promise of the American Revolution in her own life, in her support of her husband's contribution to the nation, and in the legacy of service that she passed on to her children.

Unresolved Issues

The philosophical and religious ideas that spurred the American Revolution were not able to solve all problems right away. Democracy and slavery are incompatible, yet the entire plantation economy of the South depended on slaves. Native Americans were another important issue for the Founding Fathers. In the early years of the nation, the government's policy was to assimilate Native Americans. To this end, government officials worked with church missions to teach Native Americans Christian theology, reading, and writing, along with training them in agriculture.

Although the ideals of equality and natural rights promised by the American Revolution did not fully materialize after the war, its words continued to shape the country's development. As you read about the colonists' growing independence, the immigrants' belief in America as the promised land, the women's service to their nation in wartime, and the vibrant words of Thomas Paine, think of the original intent behind those words and actions. The early Americans who offered their ideas and lives created a foundation on which today's nation still rests.

_____

_____

_____

_____

_____

_____

_____

_____

_____

_____

_____

_____

_____

_____

_____

_____

_____

_____

The New Americans

Michel-Guillaume Jean de Crèvecoeur traveled all over America, settling on a farm in Orange County, New York in 1769. Crèvecoeur celebrated the American spirit, which he found tolerant, free of class bias, individualistic, and hardworking. He ignored evidence of slavery, however, and issues of ethnic prejudice.

Another witness to the changes in the colonies was Benjamin Franklin. Franklin was partly in agreement with Crèvecoeur's perspective but did not see the colonies as all of one piece. He felt they had distinct personalities. In addition, Franklin observed that Englishmen who had settled in America had a sense of mixed allegiance due to the growing divide between their adopted and their mother country.

Initially, the development of the colonies took place mainly in New England and the Chesapeake regions. Until the 1700s, most of the American colonies were inhabited by English settlers (and, of course, Native Americans). New York was the exception because of its significant Dutch population. During the period between 1700 and 1775, the population of the colonies grew from about 250,000 immigrants to over 2.5 million. Immigrants tended, at least initially, to be drawn to areas where there were already others of their kind because it gave them some certainty of support and orientation in their new country. Immigrants came for all sorts of reasons, escaping political, religious, and economic hardships chiefly among them. The greatest number of non-English immigrants were Scotch-Irish who came from Northern Ireland.

The first settlers in Pennsylvania were primarily German. Even though they tended to stay in their own ethnic group and speak their own language, Pennsylvania, in general, became an early harbor for diversity. Pennsylvanians tolerated a variety of religious perspectives and had a productive relationship with Native Americans. The region spawned farmers, tradespeople, merchants, and shippers.

Georgia as well was different in many ways from other colonies. During the 1730s, the Scotch-Irish moved South, settling in Virginia, the Carolinas, and Georgia. Georgia was the last of the thirteen colonies to be established. Its founder, James Oglethorpe, planned to send English debtors to the new colony to relieve their unnecessary suffering in prison. He also wanted a buffer between Spanish Florida and South Carolina. Scots and Salzburgers went to Georgia as well. So did John Wesley, founder of the Methodist Church, as did the famous preacher George Whitefield. Georgia was also inhabited by Native Americans who got along well with Oglethorpe. As a planned colony, Georgia received financing from the crown. In addition, Georgia initially prohibited slavery and liquor imports. Eventually, Georgia's settlers reacted against the stringent limitations placed on them and slavery was adopted as a practical measure to develop the economy.

In addition to free immigrants, the largest group of immigrants into the colonies was enslaved Africans. The colonies offered plenty of land but there was a severe lack of labor. Therefore, landowners used both slaves and indentured servants as their labor force. Indentured servants, mostly from England, Germany, and Northern Ireland, had to work for seven years to pay off the cost of their trip. Slaves greatly increased the wealth of the Southern colonies. There were also some slaves in the Northern colonies.

Overall, visitors to the United States were impressed by its people's pride in hard work and their entrepreneurial energy. The economic trend was toward free enterprise and capitalistic accumulation. The individualistic spirit of the people complemented the nation's determination to become independent.

Notes

Use the cluster diagram to take notes about the different groups that came to the American colonies. As you put each group's name into a circle, write an important fact about the group.

Immigrant Groups

Notes

Use a compare and contrast chart to look at the differences between some of the women of the Revolution. Choose two women and take notes on their contributions.

Compare	Contrast

Women in the Continental Army

In 1780, the troops of the Continental Army were in desperate need of money, rations, and clothing. In response, Esther De Berdt Reed, the first lady of Pennsylvania, printed the following appeal. She invoked scripture, Roman history, and the history of European nationalism to justify women's "love for the public good." The appeal raised over $300,000 that bought linen to make thousands of shirts for soldiers.

PRIMARY SOURCE: BROADSIDE

from *The Sentiments of an American Woman*
by Esther De Berdt Reed, 1780

On the commencement of actual war, the Women of America manifested a firm resolution to contribute as much as could depend on them, to the deliverance of their country. Animated by the purest patriotism, . . . [t]hey aspire to render themselves more really useful; and this sentiment is universal from the north to the south of the Thirteen United States. Our ambition is kindled by the same of those heroines of antiquity, who have rendered their sex illustrious, and have proved to the universe, that, if the weakness of our Constitution, if opinion and manners did not forbid us to march to glory by the same paths as the Men, we should at least equal, and sometimes surpass them in our love for the public good.

The time is arrived to display the same sentiments which animated us at the beginning of the Revolution, when we renounced the use of teas, however agreeable to our taste, rather than receive them from our persecutors . . . Let us not lose a moment; let us be engaged to offer the homage of our gratitude at the altar of military valour, and you, our brave deliverers, . . . receive with a free hand our offering, the purest which can be presented to your virtue, . . .

END

The words of Esther Reed represent a growing degree of activism among the free white women of the Revolutionary era. Still, for a long time to come, all such initiatives remained at the level of individual action and did not blossom into an organized movement.

Women's gender was both a liability and an advantage. On one hand, the wives of revolutionaries could be targeted. On the other hand, women could use the perception of weakness to their advantage. Women provided medical help, fed the troops, ran shops back home, and warned of planned enemy attacks.

Not content to be limited to the fringes, women also fought in active duty. Prudence Wright of Massachusetts led a troop of women dressed as men. Deborah Samson (sometimes spelled Sampson) served in disguise for over a year before a wound revealed her gender. Some fought without a disguise. On November 16, 1776, when the British attacked Fort Washington, New York, Margaret Cochran Corbin assisted her husband in his cannon duties. When he was killed, she then continued firing at the British. Her fierce commitment echoed that of other valiant individuals when she said, "I am to defend this post to the very last extremity." She was the first woman to receive a pension from the United States government as a disabled soldier.

Native Americans called the courageous patriot Nancy Morgan Hart of Georgia, the "War Woman." She served as an occasional spy, but her most famous moment was in 1780. Six unfortunate British soldiers invaded her home. She fed them and got them drunk, then stole their weapons. She wounded one and killed another as her daughter kept handing her a new weapon. They held the remaining men captive until her husband came back with other Georgia soldiers. She convinced her husband upon his return to hang the captives instead of shooting them because they had bragged about killing her neighbor. At their hanging, she burst out singing a lively rendition of "Yankee Doodle."

Notes

The Power of Words: Thomas Paine

The Great Writer

Masterfully persuasive, Thomas Paine's writing conveyed forceful arguments blended with emotional appeal. After arriving in America from England, he published in 1776 a 50-page pamphlet, *Common Sense,* that pointedly told colonists they had to break with Great Britain. He made a good case—the pamphlet sold more than 500,000 copies.

The following excerpt is from Paine's *The American Crisis.* General George Washington used this pamphlet as inspiration to fortify his troops.

PRIMARY SOURCE: PAMPHLET

from *The American Crisis*
by Thomas Paine, 1776

THESE are the times that try men's souls. The summer soldier and the sunshine patriot will, in this crisis, shrink from the service of their country; but he that stands it now, deserves the love and thanks of man and woman. Tyranny, like hell, is not easily conquered; yet we have this consolation with us, that the harder the conflict, the more glorious the triumph. What we obtain too cheap, we esteem too lightly: it is dearness only that gives every thing its value. Heaven knows how to put a proper price upon its goods; and it would be strange indeed if so celestial an article as FREEDOM should not be highly rated. Britain, with an army to enforce her tyranny, has declared that she has a right (not only to TAX) but "to BIND us in ALL CASES WHATSOEVER," and if being bound in that manner, is not slavery, then is there not such a thing as slavery upon earth. Even the expression is impious; for so unlimited a power can belong only to God.

~ *END* ~

Paine and the Great Thinkers

When the American Revolution started, Paine had served as Secretary to the Commissioners sent to negotiate with the Iroquois. He was not alone in his favorable impression of the enlightened values of democracy and freedom enshrined in early Native American civilizations. Benjamin Franklin and Thomas Jefferson shared his views on that and other subjects. Franklin, a man of pragmatism and wit, was often considered the embodiment of the Enlightenment in America. Jefferson, as a believer in popular rule, pledged himself to fight "every form of tyranny over the mind of man." The profound influence these men had upon each other and their wider circles was far-reaching and would culminate in such important documents of governance as the Declaration of Independence, the Bill of Rights, and the U.S. Constitution.

Paine and the Media

Focused and stirring, Paine's arguments roused his readers' emotions. He was a model for the effective use of the mass media of his day. He created a mass audience for his message and had such a strong voice with *Common Sense* that many historians assert that, without his call to action, the Revolution might not have happened. Above all, by disseminating his material to a huge audience, he enabled colonists to become aware that they could have access to important ideas and express a political voice.

The media of Paine's time included newspapers, pamphlets, books, and speeches. Public boards offered opportunities for anyone to post opinions, and there were many independent book publishers. People heard ideas in public speeches and, since there were few other forms of free entertainment, people eagerly listened and debated new ideas. Paine's pamphlet was read all over the colonies. His legacy lives on today in all types of grassroots activism.

∽ Notes

The Spirit of Individualism

EVENTS IN AMERICAN LITERATURE

1800	1810	1820

1805 Mercy Otis Warren writes *The History of the Rise, Progress and Termination of the American Revolution*, the earliest account by an American

1809 Washington Irving publishes *A History of New York*

1814 After witnessing naval battle during War of 1812, Francis Scott Key composes "The Star Spangled Banner"

1819 Washington Irving's "Rip Van Winkle" is published in *The Sketch Book*

1824 Irving's "The Devil and Tom Walker" is published

1826 James Fenimore Cooper publishes *The Last of the Mohicans*

1827 *Freedom's Journal*, first African-American newspaper, is founded

1828 *American Dictionary of the English Language* is published by Noah Webster

EVENTS IN NORTH AMERICA

1800	1810	1820

1801 Thomas Jefferson becomes president

1803 Jefferson doubles size of United States by buying Louisiana territory from France

1804 Meriwether Lewis and William Clark begin explorations of Louisiana territory and beyond to Pacific coast (to 1806)

1807 Robert Fulton launches *Clermont,* the first steamboat

1808 United States bans slave trade

1810 The third national census records 7,239,881 people

1812 United States declares war on Great Britain

1813 In Massachusetts, one of the first temperance associations is established

1820 Missouri Compromise prohibits slavery in western territory north of Missouri's southern border and allows slavery in Arkansas territory and Louisiana

1821 Sequoyah develops a system for writing the Cherokee language

1823 President James Monroe issues Monroe Doctrine, banning European colonization in Americas

1825 Erie Canal, a 363-mile waterway linking Lake Erie with the Hudson River, is opened

EVENTS IN THE WORLD

1800	1810	1820

1804 Napoleon crowned Emperor of France

1807 British slave trade is abolished

1812 Napoleon invades Russia

1815 Napoleon is defeated at Battle of Waterloo

1819 Zulu kingdom controls southeastern Africa

1821 Mexico declares independence from Spain

1823 Beethoven completes Ninth Symphony

1830	1840	1850

1835 Ralph Waldo Emerson, Henry David Thoreau, Margaret Fuller, and others form the Transcendental Club

1837 Nathaniel Hawthorne's *Twice-Told Tales* is first printed

1838 Henry Wadsworth Longfellow's "A Psalm of Life" is published

1839 Edgar Allan Poe's "The Fall of the House of Usher" is published

1840 The *Dial* is founded by Ralph Waldo Emerson and Margaret Fuller

1845 Henry David Thoreau begins living on shore of Walden Pond (to 1847)

1846 Herman Melville's first novel, *Typee,* is published

1847 Thoreau publishes essay later known as "Civil Disobedience"

1850 Nathaniel Hawthorne's *The Scarlet Letter* is published

1851 Herman Melville publishes *Moby Dick*

1855 Walt Whitman publishes poetry collection *Leaves of Grass*

1830	1840	1850

1830 Indian Removal Act authorizes relocation of southeastern Native American tribes—including the Cherokee, Chickasaw, Choctaw, Creek, and Seminole—to territories west of Mississippi River

1833 The American Anti-Slavery Society is founded by William Lloyd Garrison

1837 John Deere produces first steel-bladed plow, which makes large-scale farming possible in heavy soil in Midwest and West

1844 Samuel F. B. Morse sends first telegraph message from Baltimore to Washington, D.C.

1848 United States defeats Mexico in Mexican War and claims land that is now Nevada, California, and part of New Mexico and Arizona

1848 Gold discoveries in California lead to first gold rush

1850 Congress passes Fugitive Slave Act, forcing officials in Northern states to return escaped slaves to owners; Compromise of 1850 is passed, which supposedly settles controversy over slavery between slave and free states

1830	1840	1850

1839 Britain and China fight first Opium War

1848 Revolutions sweep Europe; Karl Marx and Friedrich Engels publish *Communist Manifesto*

1850 Taiping rebellion in China begins (to 1864)

~ **Notes**

Celebrating of the Self

"Good men must not obey the laws too well," Ralph Waldo Emerson said. His aphorism illustrates a vital key to the American character. After all, if the original colonists had obeyed the laws, the American Revolution would never have occurred and the country might never have existed. This rebelliousness, so much a part of our heritage, reflects an essential aspect of Emerson's philosophy of Transcendentalism, America's main contribution to the Romantic movement.

In the late eighteenth century, the movement known as Romanticism sprang up in both Europe and America as a reaction to current historical crises as well as preceding cultural movements. These movements included the rationalism of the eighteenth-century Age of Reason and, especially in America, the strict doctrines of Puritanism. Romantic artists, philosophers, and writers saw the limitations of reason as embodied in the problems of industrial capitalism. Instead, Romantics celebrated the glories of the individual spirit, the emotions, and the imagination as basic elements of human nature. The splendors of nature inspired the Romantics more than the fear of God, and some of them felt a fascination for the demonic and the supernatural.

In the first half of the century, as the U.S. population exploded and the country's borders spread westward, the Romantic spirit guided writers in the United States in their efforts to capture the energy and character of the new country. Henry Wadsworth Longfellow and Washington Irving were by far the most popular writers in the country at that time. Their works exhibit a typical Romantic preoccupation with atmosphere, sentiment, and optimism.

Although Washington Irving was the first U.S. writer to achieve international fame, the first really distinctive Northern American literature came from the Transcendentalists. The philosophy of Transcendentalism, derived in part from German Romanticism, was based on a belief that "transcendent forms" of truth exist beyond reason and experience.

Ralph Waldo Emerson gave this philosophy a peculiarly North American spin: he said that every individual is capable of discovering this higher truth through intuition.

The American Transcendental movement was composed of a loosely knit group of mostly New England poets and philosophers that came to prominence in the 1830s. "Beliefs" of Transcendentalism were never formally articulated, but the followers wanted to "go beyond" the limitations of the senses and everyday experience. Their means of transcending everyday life was through the use of poetic leaps and visionary insights, by which they hoped to discover higher truths than were available through conventional means of religion and group affiliation. At Harvard's bicentennial celebration in 1836, Henry Hedge, George Putnam, George Ripley, and Emerson met to plan a symposium for persons who, like themselves, found the prevailing state of thought in America "very unsatisfactory." Their gathering, known as the Transcendental Club, resonated with like-minded thinkers and its magazine, the *Dial*, flourished from 1840 to 1844 as an important showcase for the group's writing. The formal club dissolved around 1844, and by 1855, the movement lost steam as the energy of its ideas of freedom and individualism was transferred from literary thought to abolitionist zeal.

Henry David Thoreau, Emerson's young friend and colleague, proved a prickly but brilliant embodiment of Transcendentalist ideas. Militantly turning his back on material rewards, Thoreau devoted his life to the study of nature and his own individual spirit. The rebelliousness of the American character is well illustrated in Thoreau's famous essay "Civil Disobedience," which arose from the night he spent in jail for refusing to pay a tax. According to Thoreau, "Under a government which imprisons unjustly, the true place for a just man is also a prison." In his book *Walden*, he wrote the story of the two years he lived alone in a one-room shack in the country. To this day, *Walden* remains a genuine American masterwork.

Notes

~ **Notes**

_____

_____

_____

_____

_____

_____

Another key, if distinctly independent, figure associated with Romanticism in America is Walt Whitman. Emerson championed Whitman at the beginning of his career for the ideas and style that Emerson believed were crucial to the new American poetry. Still, as influential as Whitman has been in the twentieth century, he had to wait a long time for his contribution to be recognized by the larger public. In 1855, Whitman had to print his first collection of poems, *Leaves of Grass,* himself. Able to sell only a few copies of the book, he gave nearly all of the 795 copies away. Meanwhile, in that same year, Longfellow published *The Song of Hiawatha,* which, like his earlier books of poetry, sold thousands to become a bestseller.

Thomas Moran, another of the Hudson River School of painters, found the West to be a source of sublime inspiration. The canyon of Yellowstone, *by Moran, was one of the first images ever presented to the public of Yellowstone and influenced President Grant's decision to approve an act of Congress preserving the 3500 square miles of land. Moran's painting, the first American landscape ever purchased by the American government, cost $10,000 and was put on display in the Capitol.*

Meanwhile, in the world of visual arts, a transformation similar to the literary world was taking place. In 1825, Thomas Cole launched the Hudson River School of artists. Cole was known for painting romantic landscapes of America and of the Hudson River area. Albert Bierstadt and Frederic Edwin Church were also very well-known painters of this style. As Romanticism and Transcendentalism were born as a reaction to the dominance of classical reason in literature, Romanticism and the Hudson River School developed in direct contrast to Neoclassicism in the visual arts. Neoclassical paintings were controlled, serene, and sometimes quite stiff, much like classical Greek paintings. The new works, like Thomas Cole's, were emotional pieces that focused on the beauty of nature and the individual. As such, they sought to elicit emotions from the viewer. Additionally, these painters sought to express the American landscape as a wild paradise, a new Garden of Eden, to be tamed and cultivated by the settlers. This presentation of the natural world was unlike anything European and influenced the developing image of the American spirit.

Lewis and Clark

Copyright © McDougal Littell Inc.

Since the Jeffersonian era, the American vision of exploration involved the inventory of resources hidden in the limitless paradise of the unexplored West. Meriwether Lewis and John Clark were hired by the United States government to conduct such an inventory of the land acquired in the Louisiana Purchase. They were to follow the Missouri River and its tributaries in order to find the most feasible route to the Pacific Ocean, identifying Native American tribes, and the flora and fauna along the way. Part of their job was to map the terrain and report on encounters and events. The resulting document, the *Journals of Lewis and Clark*, provides a fascinating record of their historic mission.

This entry was recorded at the beginning of the trip to the Pacific Ocean, which they reached in 1805. Their expedition helped stoke a feeling that was later called "Manifest Destiny" (or obvious fate) of the United States—the belief that Europeans possessed a God-given right to the land between the Atlantic and the Pacific Oceans.

∽ Notes

_____

_____

_____

_____

_____

_____

_____

_____

_____

PRIMARY SOURCE: JOURNAL

Journal Entry of Captain Clark

We Set out early ran on a Log and detained one hour, proceeded the Course of Last night 2 Miles to the mouth of a Creek on the Stbd. Side Called Osage Womans <Creek> R, about 30 yds. wide, opposit a large Island and a [NB: (american)] Settlement. . . . Stoped about one mile above for Capt Lewis who had assended the Clifts which is [about] at the Said Cave 300 fee high, hanging over the Water, the water excessively Swift to day, we incamped below a Small Isld. in the Meadle of the river, Sent out two hunters, one Killed a Deer.

. . . This evening we examined the arms and ammunition found those mens arms in the perogue in bad order a fair evening Capt. Lewis near falling from the Pencelia of rocks 300 feet, he caught at 20 foot.

—Captain Clark, 23 May 1804

from *The Journals of Lewis and Clark*

 ∽ END ∽

_____

_____

_____

_____

_____

_____

_____

_____

_____

_____

_____

_____

_____

_____

_____

_____

_____

_____

_____

_____

Manifest Destiny: Go West, Young Man!

The early to mid-1800s was a time of great change in the United States. On the physical side of growth, the United States was experiencing a population boom because of higher birth rates and the increasing immigration of Europeans to the new country. With rapid growth and minimal government intervention, the nation's economy was sometimes unstable. Two depressions drove citizens to explore a variety of means for supporting themselves. For many, frontier land promised an opportunity for a new start.

The nation's ideas were also undergoing change. Romanticism, once a subversive movement, had become conventional. In the works of Thoreau and the younger Emerson, Romanticism had viewed capitalistic expansion with considerable suspicion. As the 19th century rolled along, however, the individualistic emphasis of Romanticism came to provide a key rationale for the ideologies of ruthless capitalistic endeavor. Viewing themselves primarily as Romantic individualists, Americans did not believe in limits to their progress and expansion as individuals, a society, or a nation. This philosophy led directly to the nation's favorite adage, "Go West, young man!"

The belief in the limitlessness of American expansion was supported by key advances in science and technology (such as the locomotive, the rotary press, and the magnetic telegraph). This emphasis on expansion was also seen in political events, such as the annexation of Texas in 1845. Since this territory was also claimed by Mexico, calls for war arose.

In 1845, John O'Sullivan printed in the *Democratic Review* a reaction to Texas's annexation in which he argued that the annexation was but part of a divinely ordained expansion of U.S. territory and American-style democracy.

PRIMARY SOURCE: EDITORIAL

Annexation
by John O'Sullivan

Why, were other reasoning wanting, in favor of now elevating this question of the reception of Texas into the Union, out of the lower region of our past party dissensions, . . . it surely is to be found, found abundantly, in the manner in which other nations have undertaken to intrude themselves into it, . . . in a spirit of hostile interference against us, for the avowed object of . . . limiting our greatness and checking the fulfillment of our manifest destiny to overspread the continent allotted by Providence for the free development of our yearly multiplying millions.

. . .[T]here is a great deal of Annexation yet to take place, within the life of the present generation, along the whole line of our northern border. Texas has been absorbed into the Union in the inevitable fulfillment of the general law which is rolling our population westward, the connection of which with that ratio of growth in population which is destined within a hundred years to swell our numbers to the enormous population of two hundred and fifty millions (if not more), is too evident to leave us in doubt of the manifest design of Providence in regard to the occupation of this continent. It was disintegrated from Mexico in the natural course of events, by a process perfectly legitimate on its own part, blameless on ours; and in which all the censures due to wrong, perfidy and folly, rest on Mexico alone. And possessed as it was by a population which was in truth but a colonial detachment from our own, and which was still bound by myriad ties of the very heart-strings to its old relations, domestic and political, their incorporation into the Union was not only inevitable, but the most natural, right and proper thing in the world—it is only astonishing that there should be any among ourselves to say it nay.

From *The United States Magazine and Democratic Review*, July, 1845

~ END ~

_____

_____

_____

_____

_____

_____

_____

_____

_____

_____

_____

_____

O'Sullivan's text captures the popular sentiment of American exceptionalism that propelled the nation's westward expansion. While the popular doctrine of "Manifest Destiny" energized a youthful nation, it had serious ramifications for those who were not considered part of God's design, as the design was defined by men like O'Sullivan.

O'Sullivan's sense of God's unique favor had long roots. For instance, the Puritans, who first colonized the New World, believed that theirs was the only true religion. They believed that any who did not practice it were inferior, undeserving of the same treatment as those who did. Following in the footsteps of the Puritans, many people who embraced Manifest Destiny believed that to spread American democracy to people who supposedly could not rule themselves was a God-given right and moral duty. These people, of course, consisted mainly of Native Americans who were occupying the land that the whites sought. By deeming Native Americans and Mexicans unfit to rule themselves, people of the United States could see themselves as saviors of the lost people, even as they expropriated their territory, boosted their own economy, and paved the way for a prosperous future for themselves and poverty for the indigenous population.

Confident of divine approval, people began moving west. From Lewis and Clark's mapping of the Louisiana Purchase sprang multiple trails that hosted hundreds of thousands of settlers during the nineteenth century. The map indicates the various routes the settlers of the new country took.

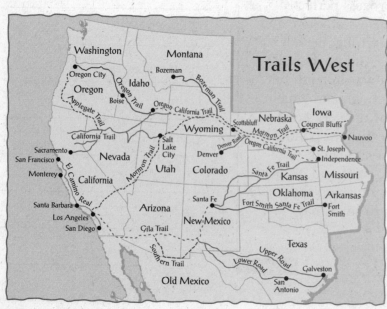

The Roots of the American Reform Movement

As the new country of the United States experienced vast expansion in territory and population, a seemingly endless series of economic crises and political scandals led some to see a need for reform. The heritage of Romanticism found expression in a surge of activity to right wrongs. Abolitionists, feminists, temperance advocates, conservationists, and labor activists all rose to address the inequities of their time, helping to cure the United States of some of its excesses and lay the groundwork for a more just society.

The Abolitionist Movement

The abolitionist movement, which began in the 1830s, advocated the immediate emancipation of all slaves. Abolitionists, including Theodore Weld, William Lloyd Garrison, Arthur and Lewis Tappan, and Elizur Wright Jr., dedicated their efforts to ending racial discrimination and segregation.

An important method of drawing the public's attention to such issues was the almanac published annually by the American Anti-Slavery Society. The Society, founded by William Lloyd Garrison in 1833, held meetings, drafted resolutions and petitions to Congress, and published almanacs, journals, and other material in its nationwide attempt to put an end to slavery in the U.S.

Articles in the Anti-Slavery Society's *Almanac*, such as the following, instructed the public in methods of civil disobedience designed to raise awareness and further the cause.

African Americans as well as whites played a vital role in the abolitionist movement. They supported Garrison's paper, the *Liberator*, and also the American Anti-Slavery Society. Frederick Douglass and other former slaves wrote and spoke about their lives in slavery and worked toward the freedom of those still enslaved.

Copyright © McDougal Littell Inc.

_____

_____

_____

_____

_____

THE

NEW ENGLAND ANTI-SLAVERY

A L M A N A C,

FOR

1841.

BEING THE 65TH YEAR OF AMERICAN INDEPENDENCE.
CALCULATED FOR BOSTON AND THE
EASTERN STATES.

" They can't take care of themselves."

BOSTON:
PUBLISHED BY J. A. COLLINS,
NO. 25 CORNHILL.
1841.

"Until the pictures of the slave's sufferings were drawn and held up to the public gaze," said Angelina Grimke in 1838, "no Northerner had any idea of the cruelty of the system, it never entered their minds that such abominations could exist in Christian, Republican America." The American Anti-Slavery Almanac was an important vehicle for spreading images of slavery and the abolitionist message.

PRIMARY SOURCE: ALMANAC

Things For Abolitionists To Do

1. Speak for the slave; plead his cause everywhere, and make every body feel that you are in earnest. Get up anti-slavery discussions in debating societies, lyceums, and wherever you can get an opening . . .

2. Write for the slave. Do you take a religious or a political paper? write a short article for it, a fact, an argument, an appeal, a slave law . . . something short and pithy . . . in short, something, if not more than five lines, full of liberty, and get them into your newspaper . . .

3. Petition for the slave. Begin at once to circulate petitions for the immediate abolition of slavery in the District of Columbia, and in Florida, against the admission of Florida into the Union as a slave state, for the prohibition of the internal slave trade . . .

4. Work for the slave. Distribute anti-slavery publications, circulate them in your neighborhood . . .

5. Work for the free people of color; see that your schools are open to their children, and that they enjoy in every respect all the rights to which as human beings they are entitled. Get merchants to take them as clerks, mechanics as apprentices, physicians and lawyers as students: if the place of worship which you attend has a negro seat, go and sit in it.

Hints To Anti-Slavery Debaters

1. Keep your temper.

2. Stick to the point, and keep your opponent to it.

3. Don't ridicule his arguments, but show that they ridicule themselves.

4. Make no random statements, prove all things.

5. Have your proofs ready, so that you can turn to them at once. Nothing tires and provokes an audience like fumbling and fumbling for what you should have at your fingers' ends.

6. Never present an argument which you are not sure is sound.

continued on page 67

7. Never degrade yourself and your subject by stooping to bandy words with your opponent, nor by playing off witticisms and smart speeches to set the audience a giggling.

8. Don't declaim but argue.

9. Don't be abstruse, far-fetched, and wire-drawn, but plain and simple . . .

10. Don't try to set off yourself, but your subject.

11. Don't leave a point till you have settled it. One point settled is better than a thousand made plausible.

12. Don't waste your time on little things, but, at the outset, seize some great point, and push it; powder spent on small game is thrown away.

From *The New England Anti-Slavery Almanac for 1841*

~ END ~

Notes

Ultimately, though abolitionists did not agree with the moderation advocated by the Republican government, they joined with them to support the Union in the Civil War. After the war, the American Anti-Slavery Society disbanded in 1870 but not without demanding land and education for the newly freed African Americans.

Early Feminist Movement

At the beginning of the 19th century, a woman in the United States did not have the right to vote or to own property. She had no rights in her marriage and no rights to her children. Women could not practice law or medicine and could not even attend college. Despite all these disadvantages, many women came together to form a united front to end such discrimination.

Women abolitionists were important and articulate members of the antislavery movement. However, even within the abolitionist movement, women found their roles limited by societal norms. Such restrictions, however, only provided greater impetus to women activists. After being denied the right to participate in the World's Anti-Slavery Convention in London (1840) because of

THE BLOOMER COSTUME.

Amelia Jenks Bloomer, a women's rights advocate and temperance activist, enthusiastically promoted the new fashion design in her temperance publication, The Lily. *While much more practical than the restrictive women's clothing of the day, bloomers, as they became known, were ridiculed by many and ultimately abandoned by feminists seeking to present a dignified image for women's rights movement.*

their gender, Lucretia Mott and Elizabeth Cady Stanton convened a women's rights convention in the United States in 1848 to address the key concerns and organize the priorities of the women's movement.

The Temperance Movement

In the early 1800s, the temperance movement organized to crusade against the consumption of alcoholic beverages. The first organized temperance association in the United States was established in 1808 in New York. By the 1830s, around six thousand temperance groups had been established. Susan B. Anthony, Frances E. Willard, and Carry A. Nation were among the most famous personalities in the fight against alcohol. In 1919, the 18th Amendment was passed banning the sale and consumption of alcohol. By 1933, however, it was apparent that Prohibition did not work and the amendment was repealed.

The Parks and Conservation Movement

As the Industrial Revolution progressed ever westward, some Americans became aware of the devastation that mining, logging and unsustainable agriculture were causing throughout the country. Writers such as George Catlin, Ralph Waldo Emerson, George Perkins Marsh, Thomas Ewbank, and Henry David Thoreau began publishing essays on preservation of the wilderness. As a result of the actions of these and other conservationists, the U.S. Department of the Interior was established. National parks were created, and laws were enacted to protect animals. For the first time, federal, state, and local governments became directly involved in the protection of American forests and wildlife.

Utopian Societies

Webster's Collegiate Dictionary defines *Utopia* as "a place of ideal perfection especially in laws, government, and social conditions." The Utopian societies of the early 19th century were based on a certain idealism, but more importantly, they were focused on organizing a community in a way that was profitable and pleasurable for all members of the community. While some communities organized themselves based on religious teachings, others on socialistic or communistic principles, all ultimately hoped to find a better way of living.

The Shakers (The United Society of Believers)

The Shakers formed one of the earliest Utopian communities. Based on the vision of Ann Lee, who believed she was the manifestation of Christ's Second Coming, the Shakers lived separate from the world and sustained a vigorous practice of religion. They got their name because they would shake and quake as they were filled with the spirit.

Founded in 1772, the Shakers were initially a small group—just Mother Ann Lee and a handful of followers. They established a communal farm in New York in 1774. At the time, they were seen as threats to the public, so they had difficulty attracting converts. However, the revivalism that started in 1776 allowed them to begin proselytizing, and by the mid-nineteenth century the Shakers had several prospering communities. Joseph Meacham, one of the first converts, led the movement to generate income by making furniture and publishing books. The Shakers continued with strong communities until the late 1800s, when the birth of industry cut down on the demand for handmade furniture and threatened their livelihood. Because Shakers were celibate and did not recognize marriage, their communities could grow only by constantly bringing in new converts. But as the nineteenth century progressed, new converts were harder to find. A few Shaker communities survived, however, and still function today.

Copyright © McDougal Littell Inc.

_____

_____

_____

_____

_____

_____

_____

_____

_____

_____

_____

_____

_____

_____

_____

_____

_____

The New Harmony Society

In 1825, Welshman Robert Owen took over an existing religious community in Indiana from its founders, the Harmonists (or Rappites, after their leader, George Rapp). As one of the most successful mill owners of the Industrial Revolution in England, Owen had introduced many humanitarian reforms in his plants and developed a new vision for society. Growing disillusioned with the slow change, he set his sights on America to establish a cooperative community. His colony, New Harmony, gained prominence as a cultural and scientific center and he was invited to speak to Congress. Settlers flocked to New Harmony, but most were unsuited to community life and unskilled in the farm or small business affairs. A feeling of dissatisfaction grew in the community and caused it to split into independent but cooperative groups. Some of these still used an entirely cooperative system, but others confined their cooperation to religion, education, recreation and work in the natural sciences, which was encouraged by Owen's partner in the venture, William McClure, a Scottish philanthropist from Philadelphia. In 1828 the community ceased to exist as a distinct enterprise, although the town remained an intellectual center. The nation's first kindergarten, first free public school, first free library, and first school with equal education for boys and girls were all established there.

Brook Farm

Emerson's friend and *Dial* editor, George Ripley, founded Brook Farm in 1841 with his wife Sophia and some fifteen members as a secular communitarian endeavor. Ripley had previously been a minister for a Unitarian congregation and sent the following letter of resignation, bemoaning the loss of care and concern for one's neighbor. At first the community thrived. Nathaniel Hawthorne was an investor and visitor. His book *The Blithedale Romance* is based on Brook Farm. Emerson and Fuller were also among the many thousands of visitors.

Eventually Ripley decided to adopt Fourierism, a socialist theory that attributed the cause of conflict and suffering to a perversion of natural human goodness by faulty social organization. It went so far as to prescribe the precise size, layout, and industrial organization of each community. Implementing such a rigid system put an end to some of the more idyllic features of life there. Because this system did not allow the community to cope well with unforeseen farming and economic problems, food shortages, and illnesses, it ultimately failed in 1847.

Oneida Perfectionists

Unlike Brook Farm, Oneida was a strictly religious community. Its founder, John Humphrey Noyes, attended a revival meeting in 1831 that inspired him to go into the ministry. At Yale Divinity School he was drawn to the doctrine of Christian perfectionism, which held that upon conversion, man attained a state of perfection (sinlessness). After claiming in front of a congregation that he himself had achieved "full salvation from sin," Noyes was branded a heretic. He then set out to publish various journals and find converts to his perfectionist ideals. He founded the "Putney Corporation or Association of Perfectionists" in 1845, which practiced his principles ("complex marriage," in which every male member of the community was married to every female, and vice versa; selective breeding; mutual criticism). Increasing local resistance—including Noyes's indictment for adultery—prompted him to relocate to Oneida. Over time the issue of group marriage again drew the ire of his secular neighbors. These tensions only intensified growing rifts within his community, which abandoned the concept by 1879 "in deference to public sentiment." But complex marriage was such an integrated part of the community life that their attempts to settle down monogamously ultimately failed. In 1881, the community dissolved and transferred its business and property holdings to a joint stock company. Their spoon factory evolved into Oneida Silversmiths, which makes flatware to this day.

PRIMARY SOURCE: LETTER

from *George Ripley's Letter of Resignation, 1840*

I cannot witness the glaring inequalities of condition, the hollow pretensions of pride, the scornful apathy with which many urge the prostration of man, the burning zeal with which they run the race of selfish competition, with no thought for the elevation of their brethren, without the sad conviction that the spirit of Christ has well-nigh disappeared from our churches, and that the fearful doom awaits us, "Inasmuch as ye have not done it unto the least of these, ye have not done it unto me."

END

∿ **Notes**

_____

_____

_____

_____

_____

_____

_____

_____

_____

_____

_____

_____

_____

_____

_____

_____

_____

_____

_____

_____

The Dark Side of Individualism

Set in an ancient castle where strange and terrifying events take place, Horace Walpole's *The Castle of Otranto* (1765) spawned the Gothic tradition in English fiction. Eighteenth-century readers fell in love with the novel's weird setting and macabre plot. Over the next century, Gothic novels of varying literary quality poured from the presses. In them, some of the greatest creatures of all time were born—including the repulsive and misunderstood monster created from human body parts in Mary Shelley's *Frankenstein* (1818) and the sinister count in Bram Stoker's *Dracula* (1897). Today, Anne Rice's sexy vampire Lestat owes his immortal life to the Gothic tradition.

The spirit and imagery of the Gothic literary tradition came in part from the Gothic architecture of the Middle Ages. Cavernous Gothic cathedrals with their irregularly placed towers and their high stained-glass windows were intended to inspire awe and fear in religious worshipers. Gargoyles—those carvings of small deformed creatures squatting at the corners and crevices of Gothic cathedrals—were supposed to ward off evil spirits. Instead, they often looked more like demonic spirits themselves. Think of the grotesque gargoyle as the mascot of Gothic, and you have an idea of the kind of imaginative distortion of reality that Gothic represents.

As noted earlier, Romanticism developed as a reaction to the rationalism of the Age of Reason. Once freed from the reign of reason, the Romantics could follow imagination wherever it might lead them. For some, the imagination led to the threshold of the unknown—the shadowy region where the fantastic, the demonic, and the insane reside. This is Gothic territory. When mainstream and optimistic Romantics looked at the individual, they saw hope (think of Longfellow's "A Psalm of Life"); but when the Gothic writers looked at the individual, they saw potential for evil (think of anything you've ever read by Edgar Allan Poe). Because of this perspective, the Gothic tradition can be called the dark side of individualism.

Psychology and the Gothic Writers

At the turn of the 19th century, people who suffered from mental illness were placed in asylums. Asylums resembled prisons more than hospitals. Because so little was known about the causes of mental illness, patients were seen as a threat to themselves and to society, so they were incarcerated and often treated brutally.

During this time, scientists were just beginning to understand the workings of the mind. Theories on how the human body and mind worked flourished, some more credible than others. In 1809, Austrian Franz Joseph Gall proposed the theory of phrenology, which was based on the premise that the bumps on a person's skull were directly connected to personality traits. Gall believed that the brain was made up of separate organs and that each controlled specific personality traits; the bigger the "organ," the more advanced the personality trait. Though his research and findings were misguided, he was one of the first scientists to link the brain to emotions and personality traits.

By 1812, the first American book on psychiatry, *Medical Inquiries and Observations upon the Diseases of the Mind,* emphasized treating those afflicted with such mental diseases as persons with an illness and not as criminals. By 1816, Johan Friedrich Herbart introduced the concept of repression, or the rejection from consciousness of disagreeable memories, events, or ideas. Though the unconscious had not yet been identified or named, Herbart's theory hinted at its existence.

Writers of the time did not need a name for the unconscious and the dark side of the human mind to explore it in their fiction. As science became clearer about the relationship between the mind and people's actions, writers became bolder about exploring the macabre and dangerous aspects of the psyche. The European Romantics' celebration of the self had evolved into an examination of the darker emotions and motivations, especially in such works as

∼ Notes

On a separate piece of paper, create a time line or sequence of events chart outlining the history of psychology. Include important developments and dates in chronological order. Show how these things affected Gothic writing.

_____

_____

_____

_____

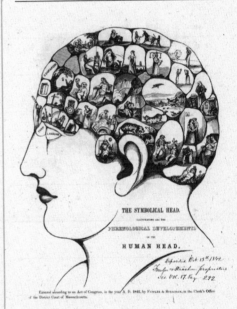

The Symbolical Head, *illustrating all the phrenological developments of the human head, was produced around 1842 by Orson Squire Fowler and Lorenzo Niles Fowler, two American brothers who were among the leaders of the phrenology movement during the 19th century. Together they formed a publishing house which produced hundreds of texts and charts on the subject, as well as cranial casts and the famous symbolical heads.*

Shelley's *Frankenstein*. In a way, Gothic writers were examining the ramifications of repression. Scientists now understand that these repressed memories, though not consciously acknowledged, do underlie people's actions. Gothic writers implicitly understood this process. American writers Edgar Allan Poe and Nathaniel Hawthorne, and to a lesser extent Washington Irving and Herman Melville, used Gothic imagery and symbolism to explore this underlying world of human emotion.

Edgar Allan Poe, the American master of the Gothic form, relied heavily on symbolism to convey various aspects of the psyche. The house deteriorating from the inside became a representation of the character's mind. Many of Poe's stories include dark, medieval castles or decaying ancient estates as setting for mysterious, strange, and terrifying events. Poe's characters are often insane; Poe himself was known to have suffered from mental illness. In the extreme situations in Poe's plots—murder, live burials, torture, and retribution from beyond the grave, characters revealed their "true" natures; and thus, greater truths about human nature. In many ways, Poe's understanding anticipated the great thinkers of psychology, such as Sigmund Freud. In "The Black Cat," Poe wrote of a "spirit of perverseness" as a primitive inner impulse, not unlike Freud's death instinct.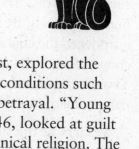

Nathaniel Hawthorne, by contrast, explored the inner workings of man's soul under conditions such as fear, greed, vanity, mistrust, and betrayal. "Young Goodman Brown," published in 1846, looked at guilt and shame in the context of a Puritanical religion. The woods became a symbol of the unconscious where dark things happened and man's primal nature emerged.

As the century progressed, theories on the human mind proliferated, providing writers with new insight and perspective on age-old human behaviors and emotions.

The Philosophy
of the Sublime

Another facet of the human psyche that intrigued and inspired Gothic writers was the concept of the sublime, which refers to a reaction a person has to an object, an event, or an idea. Think about standing and looking over the edge of a vast cliff. You may be filled with awe at its beauty. At the same time, you may feel some fear, but it is fear from a place of relative safety. In this instance, you would experience feelings of sublimity.

Edmund Burke and Immanuel Kant are two of the most prominent philosophers who discussed the sublime. In Burke's *Philosophical Enquiry into the Origin of Our Ideas of the Sublime and Beautiful* (1757), he argued that the main emotion caused by an encounter with something sublime (say a large mountain) is astonishment mixed with a little bit of fear. If something is terrible to the sight or the imagination (like a hurricane or tornado), it causes fear and astonishment. An object must have an element of obscurity, or the unknown, to cause astonishment and fear, as well as delight, and so to be considered sublime. Finally, the object, event, or idea must have a power. The power gives it the means with which to instill the sense of danger and astonishment required for a sublime reaction.

Kant takes the description of the sublime a step further in his *Critique of Judgment*, published in 1790. He divides the sublime into two categories: mathematical and dynamic. The mathematical sublime deals with size, such as a large mountain, cliff, or building. The dynamic sublime deals with power, as in the power of a storm or the idea of God. From this distinction, Kant then makes a major shift from the thought of previous philosophers. He states that the sublime is "only in the mind of the judging Subject," which would be you looking over the cliff. It is not, Kant says, a quality of the object being perceived, which would be the height of the cliff. Therefore, the

_____

_____

_____

_____

_____

_____

_____

_____

_____

_____

_____

_____

_____

_____

_____

_____

_____

_____

concept of the sublime relates to our reasoning abilities as human beings. When we first encounter something that overwhelms our sense of reason, we are taken aback (feel astonishment and fear at our limitations), but then we are able to evaluate the experience ourselves by using the object as a sort of measuring stick. Ultimately, we are able to see our "preeminence over nature" by having our reason challenged by nature and then using our reason to conceive the vastness of the immeasurable.

The sublime has been expressed repeatedly through the years in literature and art—from epic battles in classical texts, descriptions of Satan in Milton's *Paradise Lost,* to the descriptions of nature in all of its force. The rise of Romanticism lent itself well to the incorporation of the sublime. The Romantics were interested in the subjective self, exploring the passions in new ways. By exploring these passions in literary characters, American writers elicited the feeling of the sublime inspired by the vast vistas and uncharted territories of North America.

As the Romantic movement progressed, the Gothic became a mainstay. Instead of focusing on the mathematical sublime, the Gothics turned to Kant's dynamic sublime. Gothic literature builds fear in order to create astonishment and horror—but a suspenseful and delightful horror. In addition, the Gothic presents the sublime as part of the subject's reaction and not part of the object perceived. This understanding is expressed through the use of the closed-in, dark quarters that are often the setting for Gothic fiction. More importantly, the terror in the characters is often a result of the mental decay of the characters, as in Poe's "The Fall of the House of Usher."

In essence, the Gothic addresses the sublime by playing on fear itself and on fear of the unknown. Ideas are at the center of these works, expressing sublimity in the power of the human being and the unconscious. In contrast, more optimistic Romantic writers focused more externally on objects that inspired the feelings of sublimity.

The Rise of the Short Story

As familiar as the short story seems today, it is a relatively new form of fiction. In fact, it only became a specific form in the nineteenth century. Previously, stories had been told, but they were in the form of folktales originating from the oral tradition. Boccaccio's *Decameron,* which was written in the fourteenth century, was a precursor to the short story. *Grimm's Fairy Tales,* which were published in the 1820s, directly preceded the actual development of the short story as a form.

A specific definition of the length of a short story is arguable, but a workable definition is that a short story is a brief work of prose fiction. Edgar Allan Poe suggested in his 1842 review of Nathaniel Hawthorne's *Twice-Told Tales* that "the prose tale," his name for what would become known as the short story, should be long enough to be read in thirty minutes to two hours. Hawthorne had gathered together tales that he had previously published in magazines (thus *twice-told*) and had them compiled in a volume. The first printing was in 1837, the second 1841, and the third 1851.

Perhaps more important than the length of a short story is its structure. A short story has most of the same characteristics as a novel. It is just shorter. It is elaborated, like a novel, and is organized around the conflict of a plot. Because of its length, a short story should focus on "a certain unique or single effect," as Poe noted in his writing about Hawthorne, whereas a novel can present multiple layers of effects.

Short stories were exactly what magazines at the time wanted. In fact, Poe referred to the short story as the American magazines' child. *The Token, Atlantic Souvenir,* and *New England Magazine* all published stories from Hawthorne's *Twice-Told Tales.* The magazine industry was thriving and dedicated to providing its reading public with affordable entertainment. The literary quality of the contents varied from one magazine to another; however, some included works of the greatest writers of the time.

_____

_____

_____

_____

_____

_____

_____

_____

_____

Around the time that Hawthorne was publishing his volume of short stories, Poe was doing the same thing. In Poe's collection, *Tales of the Grotesque and Arabesque,* some of which had previously been published in the *Southern Literary Messenger,* he presented his first two-volume set of short stories. His stories, like Hawthorne's, were filled with the Gothic images and the spaces the human psyche explores. He did not achieve financial success with this publication. In fact, he later tried to sell the copyright to his publisher who claimed it was "worthless."

Nevertheless, Poe continued writing. He became even more creative, and yet logical, in his construction of plot. From this experimentation came well-known stories, such as "The Murders in the Rue Morgue" (1841), Poe's first detective story, which he called a tale of ratiocination. Detective fiction was suited perfectly to the process of logical reasoning, or ratiocination. By constructing such a "whodunit," Poe invited the reader, as well as the detective, to follow along the trail of clues and logic that would ultimately lead to solving the crime and the unraveling of the truth. Clues had to be presented logically, and the suspense was built step-by-step as they were uncovered.

Much of the form of detective fiction originated with Poe. Not only did he establish a quality of structure in the presentation of the clues, he also established the characters of the sly detective, his somewhat less astute sidekick, and the bumbling police detectives. Echoes of Poe's innovations are heard throughout all detective and horror fiction that has followed.

PRIMARY SOURCE: CRITIQUE

Tale-Writing— Nathaniel Hawthorne
By Edgar Allan Poe

Of skillfully-constructed tales—I speak now without reference to other points, some of them more important than construction—there are very few American specimens. . . . In the higher requisites of composition, John Neal's magazine stories excel—I mean in vigor of thought, picturesque combination of incident, and so forth—but they ramble too much, and invariably break down just before coming to an end, as if the writer had received a sudden and irresistible summons to dinner, and thought it incumbent upon him to make a finish of his story before going. One of the happiest and best-sustained tales I have seen, is "Jack Long; or, The Shot in the Eye," by Charles W. Webber, the assistant editor of Mr. Colton's *American Review.* But in general

continued on page 79

skill of construction, the tales of Willis, I think, surpass those of any American writer—with the exception of Mr. Hawthorne.

I must defer to the better opportunity of a volume now in hand, a full discussion of his individual pieces, and hasten to conclude this paper with a summary of his merits and demerits.

He is peculiar and not original—unless in those detailed fancies and detached thoughts which his want of general originality will deprive of the appreciation due to them, in preventing them forever reaching the *public* eye. He is infinitely too fond of allegory, and can never hope for popularity so long as he persists in it. This he will not do, for allegory is at war with the whole tone of his nature, which disports itself never so well as when escaping from the mysticism of his Goodman Browns and White Old Maids into the hearty, genial, but still Indian-summer sunshine of his Wakefields and Little Annie's Rambles. Indeed, *his* spirit of "metaphor run mad" is clearly imbibed from the phalanx and phalanstery atmosphere in which he has been so long struggling for breath. He has not half the material for the exclusiveness of authorship that he possesses for its universality. He has the purest style, the finest taste, the most available scholarship, the most delicate humor, the most touching pathos, the most radiant imagination, the most consummate ingenuity; and with these varied good qualities he has done *well* as a mystic. But is there any one of these qualities which should prevent his doing doubly as well in a career of honest, upright, sensible, prehensible and comprehensible things? Let him mend his pen, get a bottle of visible ink, come out from the Old Manse, cut Mr. Alcott, hang (if possible) the editor of the *Dial,* and throw out of the window to the pigs all his odd numbers of *The North American Review.*

From *Godey's Lady's Book,* November 1847.

∾ END

~ **Notes**

Conflict and Expansion

EVENTS IN AMERICAN LITERATURE

1850	1860	1870

1851 Herman Melville's *Moby Dick* is published

1852 Harriet Beecher Stowe publishes *Uncle Tom's Cabin*, increasing tension between pro-slavery and anti-slavery forces

1863 Abraham Lincoln delivers Gettysburg Address

1876 Mark Twain publishes *The Adventures of Tom Sawyer* and begins writing *The Adventures of Huckleberry Finn*

EVENTS IN NORTH AMERICA

1850	1860	1870

1851 Former slave Sojourner Truth speaks at women's rights convention

1857 Supreme Court's Dred Scott decision declares slaves and former slaves are not U.S. citizens and thus not entitled to basic rights

1854 Congress passes the Kansas-Nebraska Act creating two new territories and granting settlers the right of popular sovereignty, reopening the issue of slavery in new states and leading to violence in "Bleeding Kansas"

1859 Abolitionist John Brown is hanged for treason after leading raid on federal arsenal at Harpers Ferry

1860 Abraham Lincoln is elected president; in response, South Carolina secedes from Union, followed eventually by ten other Southern states

1863 Lincoln signs Emancipation Proclamation

1865 Civil War ends; Lincoln is assassinated; 13th Amendment to Constitution abolishes slavery

1868 Congress passes 14th Amendment to Constitution, prohibiting discrimination against African Americans

1869 California Governor Leland Stanford drives a golden spike into the ground at Promontory Summit, Utah, to symbolize the completion of the First Transcontinental Railroad in North America

1873 Colt's Manufacturing Company introduces Peacemaker revolver, most famous sidearm of the West

1874 Joseph F. Glidden patents barbed wire, key development in settlement of the West

1876 At Battle of Little Bighorn, several thousand Sioux and Cheyenne warriors defeat and kill about 200 U.S. Army troops commanded by Lieutenant George Armstrong Custer

1877 Chief Joseph of Nez Perce tribe surrenders to U.S. Army

EVENTS IN THE WORLD

1850	1860	1870

1852 David Livingstone explores Zambezi River in central Africa

1857 Sepoys rebel against British rule in India

1861 Czar Alexander II of Russia frees serfs

1867 Alfred Nobel invents dynamite; Meiji era in Japan begins period of modernization

1869 Suez Canal is completed in Egypt

1870 Italy is unified

1871 Franco-Prussian War ends; Germany is unified

1872 Critics coin term *impressionism* after Claude Monet's painting *Impression: Sunrise*

1880	1890	1900
1882 Frederick Douglass completes autobiography	**1891** Ambrose Bierce publishes "An Occurrence at Owl Creek Bridge"	
1883 Twain's *Life on the Mississippi* is published	**1895** Stephen Crane's fictional account of the Civil War, *The Red Badge of Courage*, is published	
	1897 In Pittsburgh, Willa Cather hears her first Wagnerian opera and becomes passionate fan of the German composer	

1880	1890	1900
1883 "Buffalo Bill" Cody organizes Wild West show and begins touring United States and Europe	**1890** At Wounded Knee Creek, South Dakota, U.S. soldiers kill more than 200 Sioux in last battle of Indian Wars	
	1893 Henry Ford develops gasoline-powered automobile	
	1896 Supreme Court upholds "separate but equal" doctrine of Jim Crow laws, widely used to discriminate against African Americans	
	1898 Spanish-American War results in United States gaining control of Guam, Puerto Rico, and the Philippines	

1880	1890	1900
1885 At Berlin Conference, 14 European nations lay down rules for division of Africa	**1893** France takes over Indochina	**1900** Boxer Rebellion protests foreign influence in China
	1895 Japanese defeat Chinese in Sino-Japanese War	
	1896 Menelik II maintains Ethiopian independence after victory over Italians at Battle of Adowa	

A House Divided
Slavery and the Civil War

By the time of Abraham Lincoln's inauguration as President in March of 1861, seven states—South Carolina, Mississippi, Florida, Alabama, Georgia, Louisiana, and Texas—had seceded from the Union and formed the Confederate States of America, with Jefferson Davis as President. A month later, Confederate troops opened fire on Northern troops attempting to resupply Fort Sumter, a federal installation in the Charleston, South Carolina, harbor. Three days later, Lincoln ordered additional troops to enforce the law. In response, Virginia, Arkansas, North Carolina, and Tennessee joined the Confederacy. The Civil War had begun.

Long before cannons fired over Fort Sumter, however, the controversy over slavery was tearing apart the people and institutions of the United States. Nowhere was this more evident than in America's churches. The issue of slavery caused deep divisions within the Protestant church. Staunch abolitionists took matters into their own hands and formed breakaway churches, some of which became active members of the Underground Railroad.

Anti- and pro-slavery church leaders both turned to theology to support their views. Lincoln noted, "Both sides read the same Bible, and pray to the same God." After war broke out and began to drag on, the abolitionists' conviction that God looked favorably upon the efforts of the Union grew.

Pro-slavery church leaders, meanwhile, pointed out that Abraham, the patriarch of the Jews, had owned slaves and that slavery had also existed in Jesus' time. Furthermore, in keeping with the general belief in the supremacy of white ways and dismissal of non-whites as "heathens," slaves would benefit from the exposure to the Christian principles of their masters.

Pro-slavery supporters also drew on pseudo-scientific ideas of the time to justify their views. Physiognomy, the pseudo-science of judging character and intellect based on facial features, deemed Africans a biologically inferior race.

In addition to theology and biology, social arguments were often used to support slavery. Many Southerners argued that masters and slaves were bound together by a social contract: in return for a slave's lifelong labor, a slave owner provided lifelong care, including food, housing, and medical attention.

Southerners contrasted their "benevolent" system with the system of "hireling" labor in the North. They pointed out that many Northerners could not live on the low wages they earned in northern factories or even find work at all. The hugely popular novels of Charles Dickens had made Americans aware of the problems created by the industrial revolution in England. Southerners defended the plantation system by pointing out that it avoided these problems by guaranteeing productive work and social benefits for all. They argued that slavery, in effect, established kinder relations between capital and labor.

Slavery became a major subject on American writers' minds. Often writers supported themselves with lecture tours where they spoke in front of large crowds. Henry David Thoreau's lecture, later published as an essay titled "Civil Disobedience," discussed the individual's

~ Notes

_____

_____

_____

_____

_____

_____

_____

_____

_____

Organize your thinking by using a Venn diagram to compare and contrast the issues discussed in this section.

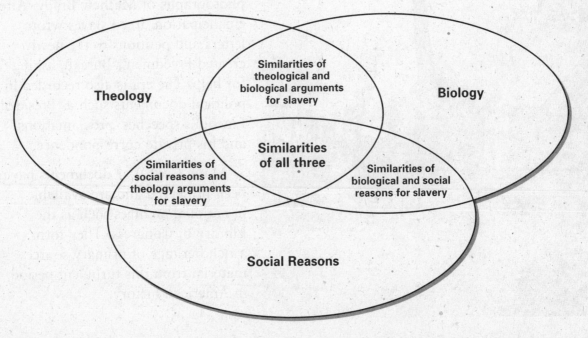

~ Notes

_____

_____

_____

_____

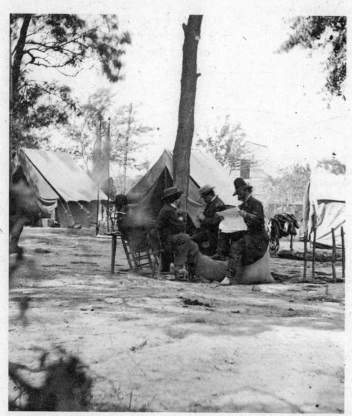

Mathew Brady was the first photographer to document with photographs the carnage of war. He oversaw a corps of photographers on the battlefields of the Civil War as they chronicled war scenes that would later shock the public. On-site photography at that time was a challenge, requiring the mixing of chemicals, the preparation of wet plate glass negatives, and the improvisation of some sort of darkroom.

responsibility to take action against unjust laws. Abolitionists also advanced this argument.

This crucial time period also generated some of the first important literature by African Americans. Frances Ellen Watkins Harper became the first popular African American poet. She traveled throughout the North lecturing on abolition and punctuating her lectures with her poetry.

Another eloquent voice of that time was that of Frederick Douglass, the escaped slave who taught himself to read and write and later became a champion of the abolitionist cause and women's suffrage.

As always during periods of great change, it is the experience of real individuals caught up in large historical forces that finally gives life to events, taking them out of the abstract into the concrete. Americans recorded their experiences during the Civil War period in countless letters, diaries, and journals. Settlers kept journals of events leading up to the war in "Bleeding Kansas." Soldiers kept journals and wrote letters home from the front to their families, or got letters from them.

Newspapers published eyewitness accounts of the war and—thanks to the new technology of photography—the battlefield photographs of Mathew Brady. After emancipation, freed slaves wrote letters and petitions to the newly created Freedmen's Bureau, asking for help. The era is also recorded in political documents such as President Lincoln's speeches, proclamations, and his private correspondence.

Many Civil War documents have been preserved and are available in national archives such as the Library of Congress. They form a rich heritage of primary source material from this turbulent period in American history.

Divisions Within the Abolition Movement

Just as the issue of slavery split the nation, there were divisions among abolitionists on how to achieve their goals. Beginning in 1831, William Lloyd Garrison used his newspaper, the *Liberator,* as a pulpit to advocate the immediate emancipation of all slaves. This was not a popular view in the 1830s, when many abolitionists worried whether the country could assimilate so many freed slaves. Garrison also believed in the dissolution of the Union because he felt that the U.S. Constitution was a pro-slavery document.

For many years, Garrison was Frederick Douglass's mentor. Douglass had heard one of Garrison's fiery speeches only days before Douglass made the public address that launched his own career as an abolitionist. Their views, however, ultimately diverged. After founding his own newspaper, the *North Star,* Douglass announced that he did not think the Constitution was a pro-slavery document and believed it could even be "wielded in behalf of emancipation."

Garrison felt betrayed and denounced Douglass in his newspaper. Harriet Beecher Stowe, author of *Uncle Tom's Cabin,* urged him to reconcile with Douglass—to no avail.

PRIMARY SOURCE: LETTER

Letter from Harriet Beecher Stowe

Cabin, Dec. 19 [1853]

Mr. Garrison

Dear Sir:

After seeing you, I enjoyed the pleasure of a personal interview with Mr. Douglass and I feel bound in justice to say that the impression was far more satisfactory, than I had anticipated.

There does not appear to be any deep underlying stratum of bitterness—he did not seem to me malignant or revengeful.

continued on page 86

～ Notes

Use a cluster diagram to list Stowe's reasons for Garrison reconciling with Douglass.

_____

_____

_____

_____

_____

_____

_____

_____

_____

_____

_____

PRIMARY SOURCE: LETTER

continued from page 85

I was much gratified with the growth and development both of his mind and heart. I am satisfied that his change of sentiments was not a mere political one but a genuine growth of his own conviction. . . .

At all events, he holds no opinion which he cannot defend, with a variety and richness of thought and expression and an aptness of illustration which show it to be a growth from the soil of this own mind with a living root and not a twig broken off other men's thoughts and stuck down to subserve a temporary purpose.

His plans for the elevation of his own race, are manly, sensible, comprehensive, he has evidently observed carefully and thought deeply and will I trust act efficiently.

You speak of him as an apostate—I cannot but regard this language as unjustly severe—Why is he any more to be called an apostate for having spoken ill tempered things of former friends than they for having spoken severely and cruelly as they have of him?—Where is this work of excommunication to end—Is there but one true anti-slavery church and all others infidels?—Who shall declare which it is. . . .

What Douglass is really, time will show—I trust that he will make no further additions to the already unfortunate controversial literature of the cause. Silence in this case will be eminently—golden.

I must indulge the hope you will reason at some future time to alter your opinion and that what you now cast aside as worthless shall yet appear to be a treasure.

There is abundant room in the antislavery field for him to perform a work without crossing the track or impeding the movement of his old friends and perhaps in some future time meeting each other from opposite quarters of a victorious field you may yet shake hands together. . . .

Very sincerely your friend,

H. B. Stowe

～ END ～

Copyright © McDougal Littell Inc.

Nativism and the Know-Nothing Party

Slavery was not the only issue dividing the country in the mid-nineteenth century. An anti-immigrant and anti-Catholic movement known as nativism flourished in the United States between 1852 and 1856.

Nativist sentiments began to emerge in the 1840s as native-born Americans became alarmed by a rising tide of German and Irish immigrants. Fleeing poverty, famine, or political and religious strife in Europe, these newcomers were disposed to gravitate toward Democratic political institutions, much to the resentment of non-Democratic old-stock Americans.

Nativists had two reasons for alarm. First, the new wave of immigrants often had no choice but to accept lower pay than native-born workers. Americans felt that their jobs were in danger. Second, many of the new immigrants were Catholics. Since many of the original Protestant settlers had emigrated to North America specifically to escape persecution from the Catholic Church, the Catholic immigrants were seen as beholden to the Pope in Rome and therefore a threat.

These nativist sentiments led to the formation of a new political party, the American party. It became known as the Know-Nothing party because its members were supposed to say, "I know nothing" when asked about their exclusive, native-Protestant organization. The party's agenda called for a law restricting immigration, the exclusion of the foreign-born from voting or holding public office in the United States, and increasing the naturalization period from 5 to 21 years.

The Know-Nothings did not become a decisive force in American politics. The issue of slavery proved its undoing and drove many of its Northern members into the new Republican party. By 1860, the Know-Nothings had disappeared, though nativism would return in other forms after the war.

_____

_____

_____

_____

_____

_____

_____

_____

Dred Scott, the former slave whose attempt to sue for his freedom resulted in the famous Supreme Court ruling that African Americans were not considered citizens and therefore had no right to sue for their freedom.

DRED SCOTT.

The Issue of Secession

Before 1850—despite their differences over slavery and other issues—few Americans were advocating secession. Several events, however, contributed to rising tensions throughout the 1850s and drove people apart.

In 1854, Congress passed the Kansas-Nebraska Act creating two new territories and giving its residents the right to decide whether or not to allow slavery within their borders. The Act served to repeal the Missouri Compromise of 1820 that prohibited slavery north of latitude 36°30'. This arbitrary divide had been an attempt to balance the power between slave and free states. The Kansas-Nebraska Act, however, reopened the question of slavery in new territories.

In response, people from opposite sides of the slavery issue rushed to settle in Kansas Territory, hoping to affect the outcome of the first election held there after the law went into effect. The pro-slavery voters carried the election but were accused of fraud. Anti-slavery voters forced another election but the pro-slavery settlers refused to vote, resulting in the establishment of two opposing legislatures. Violence soon erupted and escalated to a point where the relentless bloodshed prompted _New York Tribune_ publisher Horace Greeley to nickname the territory "Bleeding Kansas." When a subsequent election resulted in a similar controversy, Congress refused to allow Kansas to become a state.

As Kansas bled, another event contributed to the growing divisions among the people. In 1857, the Supreme Court handed down its decision in the Dred Scott case. Dred Scott was a slave who had moved with his owner to Illinois, which was a free state. Scott sued for his freedom, arguing that his slave status was nullified in a free state. His case went to the Supreme Court which ruled that all blacks—slave or free—were not and could never become citizens of the United States and therefore could not sue for freedom. The court also declared the 1820 Missouri Compromise unconstitutional, thus permitting slavery in all of the country's territories.

Finally, abolitionist John Brown's raid on a federal arsenal at Harper's Ferry further divided the nation. He was captured by Robert E. Lee, tried, and executed. Supporters hailed Brown as a hero while others reviled him as a threat to the nation.

In this atmosphere of enflamed passions, Abraham Lincoln was elected president in 1860. Although he had stated that he had no plans to end slavery in those states where it already existed, many Southerners perceived his election as a threat and the South Carolina legislature voted to secede, as did six more states.

Lincoln refused to recognize the secession as legal. He found an unexpected ally in the writer Anna Ella Carroll, a Southern woman of cultured background from one of Maryland's most prominent (and slave-holding) families.

Carroll was instrumental in keeping Maryland—a slave state—in the Union. The War Department published her arguments against secession and requested that she prepare papers on other unsettled points. Her pamphlet "The Relation of Revolted Citizens to the National Government" made the case that the secession and formation of the Confederacy were illegal. The general rebellion, she argued, was the sum of individual acts of rebellion. Once the government removed the rebels, the states would resume their former relationship to the central government. Therefore, the executive power of the president superseded the legislative power of the states. Lincoln adopted her arguments to justify exercising his wartime authority.

Carroll became one of Lincoln's trusted advisors during the war. He sent her to observe preparations for a military campaign to secure the Mississippi River. Carroll astutely saw that the Union could cut Confederate forces in two by securing the Tennessee River instead. Her plan was adopted, resulting in major strategic gains for Union forces early in the war. Her contributions, Lincoln thought, could for political reasons not be publicly acknowledged at the time. His untimely death prevented him from giving her official recognition; Congress rectified that many years later and granted her a monthly pension of $50.

~ **Notes**

_____

_____

_____

_____

_____

_____

_____

_____

_____

_____

_____

_____

_____

_____

_____

_____

_____

Reconstruction of the South and Jim Crow Laws

When the war ended on April 9, 1865, more than 620,000 men had been killed and at least that many more had been wounded. The Union had been preserved, but the South lay in ruins, and the nation now had to figure out how to integrate into American society the nearly four million former slaves.

Lincoln's assassination—only five days after Lee's surrender—effectively silenced the voice that had called for a peace "with malice toward none, with charity for all." After his death, a faction of the Republican Party, the Radical Republicans, pushed through legislation a law that, in effect, punished the South for the costly war. The Reconstruction Acts of 1867 and 1868 sent federal troops to occupy the South. There, the troops enforced new laws, including the 13th Amendment abolishing slavery, and the 14th Amendment giving all citizens equal protection under the law. This period is known as Reconstruction.

For many white Southerners, Reconstruction was a bitter time. They had to grapple with the immediate realities of poverty, hardship, military occupation, greedy opportunists known as carpetbaggers, and a changing society in which their ex-slaves were now citizens under the law. Former Confederates cultivated nostalgia for the way of life that had been taken from them. They idealized the plantation system, recalling it as a benevolent, self-sufficient society inhabited by courtly women and gallant men. These notions were reflected in the literature of the time—highly romantic novels which drew heavily on images of "moonlight and magnolias."

White Southerners began to develop the myth of the Lost Cause, the idea that the Confederacy had been a doomed, though heroic, dream. According to this myth, the South had fought not to preserve slavery, but to defend states' rights. The struggle of the Confederacy was thus memorialized in people's minds as a just and moral cause for which they were being unjustly punished.

Meanwhile, the U.S. government struggled to help former slaves make the transition into citizenry. The Freedmen's Bureau, created in 1865, provided rations and medical care, and helped people negotiate contracts with employers—who often were their former owners. The Bureau also helped finance and build hundreds of schools for African American children, staffed with teachers from Northern religious organizations.

These measures generated intense resistance from white Southerners. They reacted by enacting Black Codes, laws restricting African Americans' freedoms. These Codes ushered in a period symbolized by Jim Crow, a stereotype of a freed slave. In one state, an African American who quit a job could be forcibly returned to his or her boss. Some Codes forbade freed persons from having any jobs except those of farm worker or servant. The Codes also limited the sale of property to African Americans, imposed strict curfews on them, banned their possession of firearms, and restricted their voting rights.

Unfortunately, Jim Crow did not stop there. In 1865, former Confederate Army officers founded a secret organization called the Ku Klux Klan (the Greek word *kuklos* meaning "circle"). The Klan used violence to intimidate anyone who threatened white supremacy. By 1871, the violence was so serious that President Ulysses S. Grant used national troops to restore order in affected districts. Violence also broke out in cities as African Americans moved into urban areas, competing with whites for jobs and housing. Whites who felt threatened responded with mob attacks on black communities in cities such as New Orleans, Memphis, and Vicksburg.

Reconstruction came to an abrupt end in 1877 when the last federal soldiers were withdrawn from the South. This left African Americans at the mercy of Jim Crow violence and more or less state-sanctioned discrimination. In the end, they won their freedom but not their equality, an issue that was deferred until the 20th century.

Meanwhile, Americans had grown tired of the seemingly endless Reconstruction. Increasingly, they turned their gaze westward, where open spaces beckoned them.

∿ Notes

Use a cause and effect chart to diagram the effects of Reconstruction.

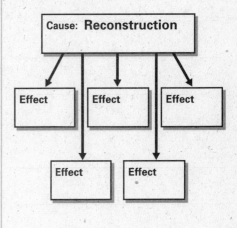

_____

_____

_____

_____

_____

_____

_____

_____

_____

_____

_____

_____

Tricksters and Trailblazers

Before white settlers in large numbers had pushed west of the Mississippi, many tribes of Native Americans populated the vast frontier. The Sioux (soo), the Cheyenne (SHI-en), the Arapaho (e-RAP-e-ho), the Kiowa (KI-e-wa), and the Comanche (ke-MAN-che) on the Great Plains had developed a way of life that depended almost exclusively on the large herds of buffalo, estimated at 15 million head in 1865. In the Southwest, the Apache had fought against the Spanish for 250 years; yet other southwestern tribes, such as the Navajo, had adopted Spanish ways and were raising sheep and goats and cultivating crops. The Nez Perce (nez purs) of the Pacific Northwest had coexisted peacefully with white traders and trappers since Lewis and Clark first explored their vast territory in 1805.

During the California gold rush of 1848, the dream of riches lured thousands of miners west. Within 30 years of that first discovery, gold or silver had been found in every Western state and territory.

By the 1860s, the plains themselves began to be settled. The Homestead Act of 1862 granted free land by turning over vast amounts of the public domain to private citizens. 270 million acres, or 10 percent of the area of the United States was claimed and settled under this Act. Newly constructed railroads transported more than 8 million settlers in two decades alone.

This relatively rapid settlement of the West doomed the Native American way of life. White settlers believed that they were bringing civilization to the wilderness, and few considered the Indians to have any legitimate claim to the land. One by one the tribes were forced—through armed conflict or signed treaties—to surrender their territories to the U.S. government. The tribes were often relocated onto cramped reservations, on land so poor that no white settlers wanted it.

Sunday April 3d 1859

After the Civil War and by the time the West was being settled, American literature was also changing. Realism replaced Romanticism as the dominant literary style, in part because people wanted to read more truthful accounts of ordinary life rather than the sentimentality of romantic fiction. The new regional diversity that sprang up among the mining camps, cattle ranches, farming communities, and frontier towns in the West gave rise to a new regional literature called local-color realism.

Camp 90 - De Cassue Creek.

Daniel Jenks, a Rhode Island native, ventured out West several times in search of gold. He documented his travels in a diary, which he later illustrated with some 20 sketches of the experience.

The era was captured in the letters and journals of settlers moving west in wagon trains. Newspapermen such as Brett Harte and Samuel Clemens published accounts of the wild days of the California Gold Rush, and miners kept journals as well. President Andrew Jackson used his addresses to the nation to explain his policies on Native Americans. Newspaper editors spoke out on the "Indian question," while Native Americans put forward their own positions in briefs filed in court cases, interviews, and letters to the United States government.

Think about the difference between the selections you find in this section and the writing of Poe, Hawthorne, and Thoreau, who wrote earlier in the century, and you'll understand how the United States' westward expansion shifted the focus of Americans' concerns.

Pilgrims on the Plains, *by Theo R. Davis, illustrates daily life in a wagon train. In 1841, the first caravan of covered wagons brought pioneers across the Great Plains, heading for California and Oregon. Within two years, more than 1,000 people had made the journey.*

∽ **Notes**

_____

_____

_____

_____

_____

_____

_____

_____

_____

_____

_____

_____

Westward Expansion and the Realities of Frontier Life

In the early 1840s, San Francisco had only a few hundred residents. Most settlers were interested in ranching or agriculture. All that changed on January 24, 1848, when James Marshall saw a glint of gold in the American River where he and 20 men had gone to build a sawmill for John Sutter. Sutter tried to suppress the discovery to protect his own interests, but stories of gold trickled out.

Soon the rumors reached all the way back east. Horace Greeley, in his *New York Tribune,* wrote, "Fortune lies upon the surface of the earth as plentiful as the mud in our streets." By 1849, tales of gold, free for the taking, in California fueled the Gold Rush—a mad stampede west. That year, thousands of "forty-niners" left for California hoping to strike it rich.

Many who set out were city-folk who had never fired a rifle or ridden a horse. Often they had no idea of how difficult the journey would be. The sea route around the tip of South America often took more than six months. A "shortcut" across Panama was equally grueling (and the Panama Canal did not yet exist). Many did not survive the overland journey on foot through the tropical rain forests of Central America. Those who did survive often had to wait in disease-infested coastal towns for a ship up the coast to San Francisco. Others crossed the country on the Oregon-California Trail. This 2,000 mile journey in covered wagons took months. Still, many eagerly set out for California.

John Swan, one of the earliest miners to try his luck in the mines, made some humorous observations in his journal about greenhorns arriving from the East Coast.

from *A Trip to the Gold Mines of California in 1848*

By John Swan

I was amused at seeing some of the machines made in New York City and sold to some of the gold seekers who came out in 1849 in the *California,* the first steamer that arrived of the line between San Francisco and Panama. Some of them were boxes . . . [with] iron grating or sieve on the top, and a drawer in the bottom. The dirt was to be thrown on the grating . . . but both dirt, gold, and most of the water went into the drawer and choked it up.

I believe none of these fancy gold machines went to the mines, though a lot of them came to California by the first steamer. No doubt the inventor made a good speculation out of it, . . . [as] they sold well to the green gold seekers who were leaving New York to come to California, though . . . none of them were green enough to take them to the mines with them after they arrived in California. The New York gold-saving machines were a great invention, but unfortunately they labored under the disadvantage of saving the dirt as well as the gold; and the miners only wanted the latter metal and were down on the machines, as they could get plenty of dirt in New York without having to come to California to get it.

But few of the miners who were camped with me in the Log Cabin Ravine or going to it are now living. Some went to the Atlantic States or Europe, and the bones of many of them are now bleaching among the gulches and ravines of the Sierra Nevada.

↜ *END* ↝

Not everyone went west to dig for gold. Entrepreneurs saw other opportunities. In ramshackle boomtowns with names like Gouge Eye and Hangtown, people made money by supplying miners with the goods and services they desperately needed. Enterprising women

↜ Notes

Use a cause and effect chart to diagram the effects of westward expansion.

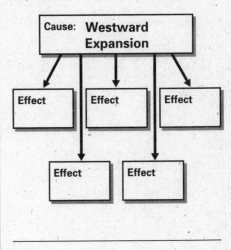

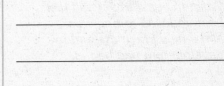

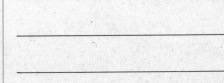

_____

_____

_____

_____

_____

_____

_____

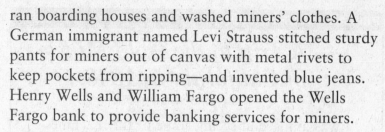

California governor, Leland Stanford, and other railroad officials rode the Jupiter to the Golden Spike ceremony. (Native Americans can be seen on the hilltop overlooking the train.) On May 10, 1869, Stanford drove a golden spike into the ground where the two lines met in the Utah territory. A telegraph message transmitted to both coasts simply read, "Done." The country erupted in celebration. Coast to coast travel had just been reduced to one week, and a new era in the nation's development had begun.

ran boarding houses and washed miners' clothes. A German immigrant named Levi Strauss stitched sturdy pants for miners out of canvas with metal rivets to keep pockets from ripping—and invented blue jeans. Henry Wells and William Fargo opened the Wells Fargo bank to provide banking services for miners.

People from other countries were also lured to the American west. During the years of 1845 to 1850, the great potato famine devastated Ireland. Half a million Irish emigrated to America, many of them drawn to California's gold. Many Chinese immigrants also arrived, hoping to send money home from the land they called "Gold Mountain." Mexicans, South Americans, Germans, French, and Turks, all sought their fortunes in California. San Francisco grew almost overnight into a bustling city that soon boasted theaters, an opera house, and more newspapers than any city except London.

Others migrated west not for gold but for other reasons. The Homestead Act that the government had passed in 1862 offered free land to anyone willing to settle the Great Plains. Many jumped at this chance. The Mormons, a religious group facing persecution in the East, set out to build a new home for themselves near the Great Salt Lake in what became the state of Utah.

As early as 1845, far-sighted businessmen saw the need for better cross-country transportation and proposed building a transcontinental railroad. President Lincoln signed a bill in 1862 subsidizing the project, and the Central Pacific Railroad company started laying tracks from the west, while the Union Pacific Railroad started laying tracks from Omaha—the western-most point of existing rail lines. Chinese immigrants made up a large part of the work force that blasted a route over the Sierra Nevada using highly unstable nitroglycerin explosives. From the east, German and Irish immigrants worked alongside Civil War veterans to lay tracks across the plains, often encountering hostile Native Americans.

Indian Removal,
Trail of Tears,
Indian Wars, and the
Battle of Wounded Knee

Early in the nineteenth century, as the United States expanded into the lower South, white settlers considered Native Americans an obstacle to progress and pressured the U.S. government to acquire Native American land. Andrew Jackson, a forceful proponent of this policy, had led U.S. troops that defeated the Creek tribe in southern Georgia, wresting 22 million acres of land from them. Jackson also fought in the wars against the Seminole of Florida.

Between 1814 and 1824, Jackson had helped negotiate nine treaties with Native American tribes that offered them lands in the west in exchange for their lands in the east. The tribes agreed to the treaties for strategic reasons but only a small number of Creeks, Cherokee, and Choctaws actually moved to the new lands.

In 1823 the Supreme Court ruled that Indians could occupy lands within the United States, but could not hold title to those lands. The Cherokee sought legal means to hold on to their lands. In 1827, they adopted a written constitution, declaring themselves a sovereign nation. The state of Georgia refused to recognize their sovereignty and the tribe took its case to the Supreme Court, which ruled against the Cherokee. The tribe appealed and, in 1831, the Supreme Court ruled in its favor. Yet, Andrew Jackson, who was then president of the United States, refused to enforce the ruling.

A year earlier, Jackson had pushed through Congress legislation called the "Indian Removal Act" which required Native Americans living east of the Mississippi River to give up their lands and relocate west. In his second annual message to congress, Jackson explained his position on Native Americans—views held by many Americans of that time.

Compare and contrast Andrew Jackson's and John Ross's positions on this issue.

Andrew Jackson	Similarities of both men's positions on the U.S. government's policy of Indian removal	John Ross

_____

_____

_____

_____

_____

_____

_____

_____

_____

_____

from *Second Annual Message to Congress*

by Andrew Jackson, December 6, 1830

The waves of population and civilization are rolling to the westward, and we now propose to acquire the countries occupied by the red men of the South and West by a fair exchange, and, at the expense of the United States, to send them to land where their existence may be prolonged and perhaps made perpetual. Doubtless it will be painful to leave the graves of their fathers; but what do they more than our ancestors did or than our children are now doing? To better their condition in an unknown land our forefathers left all that was dear in earthly objects. Our children by thousands yearly leave the land of their birth to seek new homes in distant regions. Does Humanity weep at these painful separations from everything animate and inanimate, with which the young heart has become entwined? Far from it. It is rather a source of joy that our country affords scope where our young population may range unconstrained in body or in mind, developing the power and facilities of men in their highest perfection. These remove hundreds and almost thousands of miles at their own expense, purchase the lands they occupy, and support themselves at their new homes from the moment of their arrival. Can it be cruel in this Government when, by events which it can not control, the Indian is made discontented in his ancient home to purchase his lands, to give him a new and extensive territory, to pay the expense of his removal, and support him a year in his new abode? How many thousands of our own people would gladly embrace the opportunity of removing to the West on such conditions!

~ END ~

Jackson continued his policy of negotiating treaties and using coercion to force Native Americans to give up their lands in the east and move west, but most tribes refused to move.

In 1835, a small faction of Cherokee signed the Treaty of New Echota, agreeing to relocate. Most tribe members, led by Chief John Ross, refused to recognize the treaty. The Supreme Court upheld the treaty, however, and the Cherokee were given two years to migrate voluntarily. Cherokee Chief John Ross expressed the feelings of his people in a letter to the Senate and the House of Representatives in 1836.

PRIMARY SOURCE: LETTER

from *Letter from Chief John Ross*
September 28, 1836

. . . By the stipulations of this instrument, we are despoiled of our private possessions, the indefeasible property of individuals. We are stripped of every attribute of freedom and eligibility for legal self-defense. Our property may be plundered before our eyes; violence may be committed on our persons; even our lives may be taken away, and there is none to regard our complaints. We are denationalized; we are disfranchised. We are deprived of membership in the human family! We have neither land nor home, nor resting place that can be called our own. . . .

⌒ *END* ⌒

By 1838, only 2,000 Cherokee had migrated; 16,000 remained on their land. Jackson sent in 7,000 troops who forced the Cherokee people into makeshift forts at bayonet point. There they were left to wait, sometimes for months, with little food or protection from the cold.

Later that year, Jackson ordered the troops to march the Cherokee to a new home on federal lands in Oklahoma. This march became known as the Trail of Tears because of its devastating consequences. More than 4,000 Cherokee died of cold, hunger, and disease on the way.

Under Jackson's administration, 46,000 Native Americans were moved west of the Mississippi, opening up 25 million acres of land to white settlement.

⌒ Notes

_____

_____

_____

_____

_____

_____

_____

_____

_____

_____

_____

_____

_____

_____

_____

_____

_____

_____

_____

_____

Many Lakota people embraced the Ghost Dance religion, which prophesied the restoration of Native Americans lands. The zeal of the Ghost Dance movement worried white settlers, who feared the dances could lead to uprisings; this fear influenced the events that took place at Wounded Knee.

∾ **Notes**

_____

_____

_____

_____

_____

_____

_____

_____

_____

_____

_____

The relocated Native Americans did not fare so well. Often they were isolated in poor, remote places with harsh climates. They were given little assistance in coping. General Nelson Miles, a commander of federal troops in South Dakota, protested the conditions of Native Americans in a letter to the federal Department of Indian Affairs. He noted they were close to starving, "owing to the scarcity of rations and the nonfulfillment of treaties. . . ."

In the 1880s, a new religion called the Ghost Dance spread through the tribes on the Great Plains. A Paiute mystic prophesied that a new age was coming when the earth would swallow up all whites, and Native Americans would reclaim their land of old. The wildlife of North America would return, including the buffalo, which had been severely depleted by white hunters. All Native Americans who had died would also return to enjoy a world free of their conquerors. Followers did the Ghost Dance to bring about a new era and wore shirts they thought to be bulletproof.

Lakota Chief Sitting Bull was not a believer, but he allowed his people to practice Ghost Dancing. Although the religion called for nonviolence, the federal government feared the Ghost Dance would incite new uprisings, so the War Department sent federal troops to occupy the Lakota camps with orders to arrest Sitting Bull. On December 15, 1890, as they attempted to arrest him, a gun battle broke out, and Sitting Bull and eight other Lakota were killed in the crossfire.

Fearing further reprisals, some Lakota fled to a Sioux camp led by Big Foot, Sitting Bull's half-brother. On December 23, under cover of night, the sick and aging Big Foot set out with a group of 120 men and 230 women and children on a 150-mile trek through the Badlands to reach the Pine Ridge Agency and the protection of Chief Red Cloud. Both Big Foot and Red Cloud reportedly wanted peace with the whites.

On December 28, the group was surrounded by Major Samuel M. Whitside and 500 troops from the Seventh Cavalry (once led by General George Custer) on the banks of Wounded Knee Creek. The troops had mounted cannons on both sides of the valley. A rumor ran through the tribe that they were to be deported to Oklahoma. On edge, the troops confiscated all the group's firearms. When a gun went off accidentally, the cavalry opened fire. Hearing the shots, troops stationed on the hilltops fired the cannons, turning the scene into a massacre. Bodies retrieved, after a blizzard, included many women and children, frozen and clinging to each other. Twenty-nine soldiers died, probably caught in "friendly" crossfire. Twenty-three soldiers received the Congressional Medal of Honor for their actions.

Lakota chief Black Elk witnessed the aftermath of the massacre as a young man. Years later he recorded his memories in interviews with John G. Neihardt, who published them under the title *Black Elk Speaks*.

Although many Americans were outraged by news of the Battle of Wounded Knee, others felt the government's actions were justified. One of these was Frank L. Baum, a newspaper editor in Aberdeen, South Dakota. Baum, who later became famous as the author of *The Wizard of Oz*, published this editorial advocating the extermination of Native Americans.

The Battle of Wounded Knee was the last major confrontation between Native Americans and the United States military in the nineteenth century. It brought to a sad close a painful chapter in American history, and heralded the beginning of a difficult period for Native Americans relegated to federal reservations. At the same time, however, in 1900, the United States stood poised at the beginning of a new century and a period of unprecedented development and growth.

Notes

_____

_____

_____

_____

_____

_____

_____

PRIMARY SOURCE: EDITORIAL

Wounded Knee Editorial
by Frank L. Baum, January 3, 1891

The peculiar policy of the government in employing so weak and vacillating a person as General Miles to look after the uneasy Indians, has resulted in a terrible loss of blood to our soldiers, and a battle which, at best, is a disgrace to the war department. There has been plenty of time for prompt and decisive measures, the employment of which would have prevented this disaster.

The PIONEER has before declared that our only safety depends upon the total extirmination of the Indians. Having wronged them for centuries we had better, in order to protect our civilization, follow it up by one more wrong and wipe these untamed and untamable creatures from the face of the earth. In this lies safety for our settlers and the soldiers who are under incompetent commands. Otherwise, we may expect future years to be as full of trouble with the redskins as those have been in the past . . .

from the *Aberdeen Saturday Pioneer*

END

The Changing Face of America

EVENTS IN AMERICAN LITERATURE

1855	1867	1880

1856 *New York Tribune* publishes letters by Margaret Fuller about her travels in Europe, making her America's first woman foreign correspondent

1862 Emily Dickinson writes 366 poems within the year

1869 Louisa May Alcott completes writing of *Little Women*

1870 Bret Harte publishes story collection *The Luck of Roaring Camp, and Other Sketches*

1883 Emma Lazarus writes sonnet "The New Colossus," dedicated to Statue of Liberty

1890 Charlotte Perkins Gilman writes "The Yellow Wallpaper," which describes the emotional and intellectual decline of a young wife and mother

EVENTS IN NORTH AMERICA

1855	1867	1880

1857 Elizabeth Blackwell establishes New York Infirmary for women and children, the first medical clinic of its kind

1870 John D. Rockefeller founds Standard Oil Company

1872 Susan B. Anthony is arrested and fined for leading a group of women to test their right to vote

1876 Alexander Graham Bell patents first telephone

1879 Thomas Edison invents first practical light bulb

1881 Clara Barton founds the American Red Cross

1882 Congress passes Chinese Exclusion Act, suspending Chinese immigration for ten years

1883 First metal-framed skyscraper, ten stories high, is built in Chicago

1885 Home Insurance Building is completed in Chicago, considered by many to be the first skyscraper

1886 Statue of Liberty is dedicated in New York Harbor; trade unionists organize American Federation of Labor (AFL)

EVENTS IN THE WORLD

1855	1867	1880

1855 Florence Nightingale, British nurse, introduces hygiene standards into military hospitals during Crimean War

1856 Two states of Australia introduce modern secret-voting procedure known as Australian ballot

1868 Remains of Cro-Magnon man discovered in Europe

1870 After a troubled reign, Queen Isabella II of Spain abdicates throne in favor of her son, Alfonso XII

1885 Karl Benz of Germany builds single-cylinder engine for motor car

1889 **1903** **1915**

1893 Paul Laurence Dunbar publishes first volume of poetry, *Oak and Ivy*, while working as elevator operator

1897 Edward Arlington Robinson publishes "Richard Cory"

1898 Henry James publishes *The Turn of the Screw*

1899 Kate Chopin publishes her novel, *The Awakening*

1911 Edith Wharton publishes the tragic novel *Ethan Frome*

1914 Carl Sandburg writes the poem "Chicago," an energetic celebration of life early in the 20th century

1915 Edgar Lee Masters writes "Lucinda Matlock," part of *Spoon River Anthology*

1922 F. Scott Fitzgerald publishes short story "Winter Dreams"

1925 Eugene O'Neill publishes *Desire Under the Elms,* a play based on a Greek tragedy that explores family conflicts

1889 **1903** **1915**

1889 Jane Addams opens the doors of Hull-House in Chicago

1892 Ellis Island in New York Harbor becomes chief U.S. immigration station

1895 Booker T. Washington gives "Atlanta Compromise" speech, urging African Americans to take up vocational trades

1898 Spanish-American War begins in the Caribbean

1901 President McKinley is assassinated

1903 Near Kitty Hawk, North Carolina, Orville and Wilbur Wright make first flight in engine-powered airplane

1907 Japan limits emigration to U.S. in response to hostility toward Japanese laborers

1913 Ford Motor Company puts first moving assembly line into place and is soon producing 1,000 Model T automobiles a day

1916 Margaret Sanger opens the first birth control clinic in Brooklyn, New York

1920 Ratification of the 19th Amendment gives women the right to vote

1924 Ending centuries of nearly open admissions, Congress passes Immigration Act of 1924 that limits number of immigrants from outside of Western Hemisphere

1889 **1903** **1915**

1893 New Zealand becomes first country to grant women suffrage

1896 Italian physicist Guglielmo Marconi creates first radio

1898 Pierre and Marie Curie discover radium and polonium

1901 After 64 years as ruler of Great Britain, Queen Victoria dies

1903 Emmeline Pankhurst founds Women's Social and Political Union in England to further woman suffrage

1912 "Unsinkable" English ship *Titanic* sinks on maiden voyage, killing 1,513; African National Congress formed in South Africa

1914 World War I breaks out in Europe

1915 Albert Einstein postulates general theory of relativity

1918 Women aged 30 and over gain suffrage in England

1919 Gandhi becomes leader of Indian independence movement

The Progressive Era and Women's Voices

"The power of a woman is her refinement, gentleness and elegance; it is she who makes etiquette, and it is she who preserves the order and decency of society. Without women, men soon resume the savage state, and the comfort and the graces of the home are exchanged for this misery of the mining camp." This quotation from a popular book of etiquette in 1880 voiced the widely held notion that a woman's place in society was to be "the bearer of civilized values against the animalistic forces of masculinity." That notion of women and their place in society was soon to change.

This book of etiquette advised women during the "Gilded Age" (ca. 1865–1900). That term was coined by Mark Twain, and his choice of "gilded" rather than "golden" emphasized the showiness and superficiality of the newly rich in the United States. In other words, Twain was mocking the industrialists who had made their money after the Civil War and spent their wealth recklessly on lavish parties, expensive clothes, and grandiose mansions. Industrialists such as John D. Rockefeller, Cornelius Vanderbilt, John B. Duke, and J. P. Morgan had made their wealth ruthlessly by paying meager wages and rooting out competition in such industries as steel, oil, tobacco, sugar, and iron. Working men and women, immigrants, and African Americans—among others—struggled to lead even a marginal existence. Their poor working and living conditions cried out for relief.

During the years that followed the Gilded Age, the Progressives answered that cry. The Progressive Movement was made up of educated activists who wrote for newspapers, established settlement houses, took photographs, and ran for public office. They campaigned against lynchings, filthy prisons, slum landlords, and child labor. At the same time they campaigned for social justice, universal education, and an eight-hour work day.

Despite the superficiality of the Gilded Age, signs of the coming Progressive Movement began to appear during that time. The movement to give women the right to vote had reemerged after a period of inactivity during the years of the Civil War. Nearly two million African American women, who had been enslaved, were now emancipated along with their fathers, brothers, and husbands. As suffragists wrestled with the question of whether to focus first on the voting rights of African American males before fighting for the women's vote, the matter was settled by the introduction of the 15th Amendment in 1878. This Amendment ensured the right to vote regardless of race, color, and previous servitude. But it did not address the issue of gender.

Both before and after the war the woman's suffrage movement was only the most public aspect of a growing force to give women a voice in both politics and literature. The speeches of women's activist Sojourner Truth eloquently articulated the realities of women's lives, especially the lives of African American women. At one women's rights convention, she responded to a male critic with words that resonated in the hearts of many 19th-century women:

> That man over there says that women need to be helped into carriages, and lifted over ditches, and to have the best place everywhere. Nobody ever helps me into carriages, or over mud puddles, or gives me any best place! And ain't I a woman? Look at me! Look at my arm! I have ploughed, and planted, and gathered into barns, and no man could head me. And ain't I a woman?

Although middle- and upper-class white women did not face the harsh struggles endured by women like Sojourner Truth, they faced social barriers to education and fulfillment. During the Gilded Age, some of these barriers began to fall as university education became somewhat more available to women from genteel backgrounds. Women became trained as social workers, journalists, scientists, doctors, and even engineers. Popular newspapers of the 1890s, however,

∾ Notes

_____

_____

_____

_____

_____

_____

_____

_____

_____

_____

Political cartoons about the suffrage movement illustrated society's concerns about changing gender roles as well as specific political events.

trumpeted the dangers of such advances in articles such as: "Are We Destroying Woman's Beauty? The Startling Warning of a Great English Physician Against Higher Education of Women; How Intellectual Work Destroys Beauty." In spite of this backlash, women such as Jane Addams, Ellen Gates Starr, Ida B. Wells, Clara Barton, and Dr. Susan La Flesche (later Picotte) focused on women's careers and service. Meanwhile, women authors such as Kate Chopin (*The Awakening*) and feminist activists such as Charlotte Perkins Gilman focused on personal liberation. In their work, they explored such matters as passion, repression, and male domination.

In 1920, the 19th Amendment to the Constitution gave women the right to vote. Later that year and in subsequent years, a few women assumed significant appointments in government. Suffrage heralded, however, no great revolution. Women did not unite at the polls to gain reforms for themselves; instead, many voted like their fathers or husbands, or didn't vote at all. This political failure combined with the cultural changes that rocked the 1920s—such as the rise of advertising, Hollywood glamour, and the flapper image of women—served to delay women's intellectual and literary development. The playwright Lillian Hellman, one of the few commercially successful American women writers in the 1930s and 1940s, summed up her generation this way: "By the time I grew up, the fight for the emancipation of women, their rights under the law, in the office, in bed, was stale stuff. My generation didn't think much about the place or the problems of women."

The legacy of 19th-century women lives on in the richness and diversity of contemporary life and literature. Women of all ages and ethnic groups are working in a variety of professions as well as writing and publishing literature today, and so give voice to a multitude of experiences and concerns.

The Progressive Era

The Gilded Age was a time of business expansion and considerable political corruption in the United States. The subsequent Progressive Era (ca. 1900 to 1917) was a time of reform that sought to regulate business and eradicate political corruption. A generation of socially minded women and men had actively fought for women's right to vote and the abolition of slavery before the Civil War. By the early 1900s, another generation of women and men found ways to fight corruption through the Progressive Movement. Fast growth as well as an economic depression from 1893 to 1897 exposed problems with unregulated capitalism. The rich industrialists (the so-called "gilded") wielded great power as they scrambled to amass even greater wealth. Meanwhile, the poor languished in rural poverty and city slums, often working twelve to sixteen hours a day at tedious and dangerous jobs. Progressivism sought not to end capitalism but to reform its abuses. Progressives fought for many reforms: economic, labor, political, and social.

Economic and Labor Reforms

Economic consolidation, which occured through monopolies, trusts, and mergers, allowed industrialists in the key industries of railroads, steel, tobacco, and oil, to stifle competition and to gain unfair advantage. President Theodore Roosevelt, known as a "trust buster," fought J. P. Morgan to regulate the railroads. He filed suits against John D. Rockefeller's oil trust and "busted" John B. Duke's hold on the tobacco industry. In spite of his efforts, when Roosevelt left office in 1909, nearly half of all manufactured goods came from 1 percent of American companies, giving these companies unprecedented economic, political, and cultural power.

To counteract that strength, organized labor sought to build up power of its own. Samuel Gompers, president of the American Federation Labor that represented 1.5 million members, did not wish to "bust" trusts. Instead, he offered labor as a strong

~ **Notes**

As you read this selection, think how economic consolidation may have led to economic and social abuses. In the chart below, write in the effects of economic consolidation.

counter organization. In 1907 he said: "The trade union, through association, makes production more effective, but unlike the trust it does not seek a monopoly of the benefits for the few. The trade union ever seeks to distribute the benefits of modern methods of production among the many."

In essence, Gompers maintained that both the industrial trust and the trade union were modern forms of consolidation that should be accepted as inevitable. Not all Progressives agreed with Gompers about this inevitability. However, Gompers's use of the terms "effective" and "modern methods of production" point to other beliefs with which most progressives would agree: beliefs in science, efficiency, and professional expertise to solve problems.

Political Reforms

While Progressives had faith in professional expertise, they did not have much faith in politicians. Many local politicians had made deals with the rich, consolidating their own wealth and power into organizations called "machines." At the National Social and Political Conference, held in Buffalo in 1899, labor leaders Gompers and Eugene Debs, along with social activist Florence Kelley, all called for these political reforms: direct legislation, equitable taxation, and public ownership of utilities. By direct legislation, they meant such measures as the *recall* (by which citizens could remove corrupt officials before their term was over) and the *referendum* (by which citizens could vote directly on important issues). With fair taxation, reformers hoped to remove corporate tax shelters. Public ownership of utilities would loosen the hold monopolies had on citizens' daily lives that caused excessively high fares and rates for transportation and electricity, and diminished economic opportunities and options for small businesses, laborers, and consumers.

Social Reforms

The economic and political abuses of the Gilded Age resulted in social abuses that were primarily directed at African Americans or immigrants. In his "Atlanta Compromise" speech of 1895, African American educator Booker T. Washington spoke to the Cotton States and International Exposition in response to what some called "the Negro problem." Much of "the Negro problem" had to do with abysmal living and working conditions that were the direct result of institutionalized racism. Part of it had to do with direct violence: voter intimidation, beatings, and lynching. During Reconstruction, the first Ku Klux Klan had organized in the South in order to scare African Americans into submission. Later, white rifle clubs and vigilantes romanticized the Klan as part of the tragic Lost Cause of the South, all the while carrying on the Klan's violence and terrorism. In 1915, a reorganized Klan emerged.

In response to such conditions, Washington urged those of his race to present themselves as humble and unthreatening instead of insisting on full equality. He urged African Americans to take up trades in domestic service, mechanics, and agriculture. Washington practiced what he preached and established in 1881 the nationally famous Tuskegee Normal and Industrial Institute. Washington's progressive opponent was W. E. B. DuBois, the gifted African American civil rights leader, who argued against Washington's "gradualism" and called for the most talented African Americans to fight for social justice immediately.

Meanwhile, recent immigrants from southern and eastern Europe lived in horrific conditions, in crowded tenement housing in urban areas like New York and Chicago. Women and children often huddled over the kitchen table in their tenement doing piece work—such as assembling paper flowers or cracking nuts or crocheting lace collars—for large manufacturers that paid meager fees per piece. Daily salaries were often less than a dollar for an entire family.

Progressive social workers Jane Addams and Ellen Gates Starr joined the settlement house movement to fight such slum conditions. To their Hull-House in Chicago, immigrants brought their children to daycare and to learn to read and write. By slowly improving their lives, immigrants hoped their children would be able to share in America's wealth and truly participate in the American Dream.

∾ **Notes**

_____

_____

_____

_____

_____

_____

Children in alley of New York tenements in 1912.

∽ **Notes**
Use a cluster chart to diagram
the advancements in women's
education.

Expanding Opportunities

The American Dream, in part, meant finding opportunities to improve oneself economically. For young women of the upper middle class, however, such as Jane Addams, the dream specifically meant finding opportunities to improve oneself intellectually and to find work serving society. In founding Hull-House, she and her long-time friend Ellen Star Gates chose a life of service and intellectual engagement over the more traditional roles of marriage, family, and socializing. As educational opportunities expanded in the 19th centuries, more and more women eschewed traditional life paths and emerged as pioneers in diverse fields.

Education for Women

Emma Willard was a school teacher and the first American woman publicly to support higher education for women. Her pamphlet "An Address to the Public . . . Proposing a Plan for Improving Female Education" aptly described women's goal for education in the early 1900s: "Education should seek to bring its subjects to the perfection of their moral, intellectual and physical nature: in order that they may be of the greatest possible use to themselves and others." Willard wrote the pamphlet in 1819 in order to request state funding from the New York legislature for a secondary school for girls. The legislature refused her request. Undeterred, Willard raised private funds and opened Troy Female Seminary in 1821.

After one generation had struggled to provide girls with a secondary education, the next generation struggled to provide young women with a college education. In 1833, Oberlin College opened its doors promising to give "the misjudged and neglected sex all the instructional privileges which hitherto have unreasonably distinguished the leading sex from theirs." Not only did the college commit itself to female education but also to education for all races. When Georgia Female College (later known as

Wesleyan College) opened in 1838, it offered courses to white women in Latin, mathematics, and science. Other colleges soon followed, so that by 1877 when Jane Addams attended Rockford Seminary (soon to become Rockford College) she had a respectable number of colleges from which to choose.

Pioneers in Medicine

As they became more educated, women made their way into a wide variety of fields including engineering, journalism, social work, and medicine. In 1849 Elizabeth Blackwell became the first female medical doctor in the United States. She stands out not only as a pioneer doctor but also as a forerunner of the progressive spirit, having set up her practice to serve the immigrants and the poor of New York. Other women, including her own sister, Emily, followed in her footsteps.

Well-known women of medicine during the Progressive Era include Clara Barton, founder of the American Red Cross (1881) and Dr. Susan La Flesche (later Picotte). Dr. La Flesche was the first Native American graduate of Woman's Medical College in Pennsylvania. She served her people, the Omaha, for many years (beginning in 1890) on a reservation in Nebraska. Margaret Sanger, the former nurse and midwife who fought for birth control, became an icon of the Progressive Era in medicine. In 1916, Sanger opened up the first birth control, clinic in the United States in Brooklyn. Authorities soon shut down the clinic, however, imprisoning Sanger and her sister for dispensing "obscene materials." Still, Sanger managed to educate women and doctors about the benefits of limiting pregnancies to a number that a woman's "health could stand."

Notes

Use a cluster diagram to organize the information on pioneers in the field of medicine.

_____

_____

_____

_____

_____

_____

_____

_____

_____

_____

_____

_____

_____

_____

_____

_____

_____

_____

_____

_____

_____

_____

_____

_____

_____

_____

_____

_____

_____

_____

_____

_____

_____

The Right to Vote and the 19th Amendment

Although by 1900 more and more women had proven their intelligence in school, their civic responsibility in social causes, and their capability in careers, no woman was allowed to vote. The Suffragist Movement in the United States, begun before the Civil War, slowed down during the war and then gained momentum, culminating with the passage of the 19th Amendment in 1920.

Suffragist Movement: Early Efforts

"As we reached different crossroads, we saw wagons coming from every part of the country, and long before we reached Seneca Falls we were a procession," noted glove sewer Charlotte Woodward. She was recalling her trip to the first women's rights convention. Abolitionists Elizabeth Cady Stanton and Lucretia Mott had issued the call for a meeting. Both women believed that women were not always treated with the respect that they deserved within the abolition movement as well as in society in general. They hoped a convention of women might clarify women's needs and direction. At the convention at the Wesleyan Methodist Church in Seneca Falls in 1848, Elizabeth Cady Stanton drafted the Declaration of Sentiments, part of which appears below. The echoes in Stanton's declaration of Thomas Jefferson's *Declaration of Independence* added force to the women's demands. Stanton protested women's disenfranchisement as well as their lack of property rights. Women at that time could not legally keep their wages or even their own children. They were expected to be sexually faithful and chaste while men were allowed much greater latitude.

Among the 300 who attended the Seneca Falls convention was African American abolitionist Frederick Douglass, who spoke up in support of a resolution calling for women's right to vote. This resolution was so controversial and radical at the time that it only narrowly passed. Voting rights for women would take over 70 more years to achieve. Only one woman attending the Seneca Falls convention, Charlotte Woodward, would still be alive to vote after the 19th Amendment was finally ratified.

Most of the media and the general public mocked and ridiculed the women's efforts. In the *New York Tribune*, however, Horace Greeley wrote with appropriate respect as he reported on the convention. Other women's conventions followed, including one in Worcester, Massachusetts (1850) in which a resolution demanded suffrage for both sexes and all races, and one in Akron, Ohio (1851) in which Sojourner Truth presented her famous "And Ain't I a Woman?" speech, proving to be, in the words of another feminist, a "terrible force, moving friend and foe alike."

Suffragist Movement: Later Efforts

As the United States prepared for the Civil War, activists turned their attention to the issue of slavery while the efforts to secure universal suffrage slowed down. Nearly two million black women were held in slavery in 1860. After the war secured the freedom of these women, activists turned their efforts again to voting issues. At this juncture, a potential division presented itself. Should efforts be focused on newly liberated black men, emphasizing their right to vote, or should efforts remain focused on suffrage for all?

Copyright © McDougal Littell Inc.

PRIMARY SOURCE: POLITICAL DOCUMENT

from *Declaration of Sentiments*
by Elizabeth Cady Stanton, 1848

We hold these truths to be self-evident: that all men and women are created equal; that they are endowed by their Creator with certain inalienable rights; that among those rights are life, liberty, and the pursuit of happiness . . . Whenever any form of government becomes destructive of these ends, it is the right of those who suffer from it to refuse allegiance to it, and to insist upon the institution of a new government. . . . [And] when a long train of abuses and usurpations, pursuing invariably the same object evvinces a design to reduce them under absolute despotism, it is their duty to throw off such government, and to provide new guards for their future security. Such has been the patient sufferance of the women under this government, and such is now the necessity which constrains them to demand the equal station to which they are entitled. . . .

Resolved, That all laws which prevent woman from occupying such a station in society as her conscious shall dictate, or which place her in a position inferior to that of man, are contrary to the great precept of nature, and therefore of no force or authority. . . .

Resolved, That it is the duty of the women of this country to secure to themselves their sacred right to the elective franchise.

ᔓ *END* ᔓ

ᔓ **Notes**

_____

_____

_____

_____

_____

∽ Notes

Use a chart like the one below to compare and contrast African American and white suffragists.

Compare	Contrast

_____

_____

_____

_____

Women suffragists picketing in front of the White House in February 1917.

Sojourner Truth spoke for the rights of women in this debate: "I have a right to have just as much as a man. There is a great stir about colored men getting their rights, but not a word about the colored women." Other African American women, such as Frances Watkins Harper, however, felt the issue of race, not gender, was more important. Meanwhile, some northern white women, such as Elizabeth Cady Stanton and Susan B. Anthony, at times aligned themselves with racist positions that pitted educated white women against uneducated African American males and immigrants. Southern white journalist Rebecca Latimer Felton championed the right to vote along with other social causes such as prison reform and prohibition. At the same time, Felton maintained conservative racial views, often inciting fear of "African American rapists" in a newspaper column she wrote for the *Atlanta Journal*. Felton's views contrasted sharply with those of Ida B. Wells, another southern woman journalist. Known as a key African American anti-lynching activist, Wells exposed many rape accusations as bogus.

These debates changed course with the passing of the 15th Amendment in 1870. That Amendment secured the right to vote without consideration of "race, color, or previous condition of servitude." The omission of the word sex from the Amendment made a victory for women all the more urgent. In 1878, Stanton and Anthony first presented the "Anthony Amendment" before Congress. For 41 years, it was reintroduced, every year, until in 1920 it finally became the 19th Amendment to the U.S. Constitution. This important Amendment states simply that the rights of citizens "to vote shall not be denied . . . on account of sex."

MR. PRESIDENT HOW LONG MUST WOMEN WAIT FOR LIBERTY

MR. PRESIDENT WHAT WILL YOU DO FOR WOMAN SUFFRAGE

The American Dream

In the United States, the closing decades of the 19th century were a time of rapid change and sharp contrasts. Great entrepreneurs—such as Andrew Carnegie, J. P. Morgan, John D. Rockefeller, and Cornelius Vanderbilt—amassed vast fortunes by exploiting cheap labor in the cities and creating giant companies that controlled entire industries. Urban manufacturing centers swelled with the influx of immigrants from Europe and people from rural areas in search of work. Almost half of the U.S. population was crowded in about a dozen cities, and the majority of all U.S. workers were industrial laborers sweating in factories.

As the new century dawned, the belief in America as a unique place where work and merit rather than social privilege determined one's fate remained a powerful ideal. Everyone knew of Abraham Lincoln's rise from his early life in a simple log cabin in rural Illinois. Many also knew that the millionaire newspaperman Joseph Pulitzer had come to America as a poor young German-speaking immigrant who was recruited to fight in the Civil War. People told and retold stories of those people who rose through their own efforts from humble beginnings to achieve great success.

For many writers, however, the flaws hidden beneath the optimistic simplicity of this ideal became a preoccupation. In the novel *Sister Carrie*, Theodore Dreiser challenged the notion of self-improvement by depicting a heroine first crushed, then enriched, by forces she cannot control. In *The Jungle*, Upton Sinclair exposed the appalling working conditions of immigrants in the Chicago stockyards. The poet and folksinger Carl Sandburg presented the seamy side of urban industrialization—the poverty, the crime, the corruption— even as he celebrated the courage and resilience of everyday men and women facing these blights.

The same preoccupation with the underside of the ideal also drove photographer Lewis Hine to document child laborers and sweatshops. When Hine traveled the country visiting factories, he measured the height of the buttons on his shirt so that he could inconspicuously estimate the height and age of the children he photographed as they blew glass, picked slate, or changed bobbins in glass shops, coal mines, and textile factories.

Photo by Lewis Hine: "Mrs. Lucy Libertine and family: Johnnie, 4 years old; Mary, 6 years; Millie, 9 [?] years, picking nuts in the basement tenement, 143 Hudson St. Mary was standing in the open mouth of the bag holding the cracked nuts (to be picked), with her dirty street shoes on, and using a huge, dirty jackknife . . . They live in the dark inner bedrooms, and filth abounds in all the room and in the dark, damp entry." A family such as theirs would work long hours, seven days a week, making from $1.50 to $2.00 a week for their effort.

∾ Notes

_____

_____

_____

_____

_____

_____

Edgar Lee Masters and Edwin Arlington Robinson were two poets who turned their gaze away from the cities to focus on the changes surging through rural areas at this time. Each investigated, in a different way, the currents of discontent running beneath the surface of seeming stability of small-town life. Paul Laurence Dunbar, the first African American to earn his living solely by his writing, criticized America's picturesque veneer by exposing in poems like "We Wear the Mask" the truth behind popular racial stereotypes of the day.

The American dream of material success was nowhere so minutely explored as in the stories and novels of F. Scott Fitzgerald. Nearly all of his works concern the tension between the very wealthy and those who, like Fitzgerald himself, were attracted to them. In following the lives of characters whose fates are determined by their responses to wealth and to those who possess it, he presented intimate insights into the American preoccupation with money.

For the more than 20 million immigrants who came to America in the years between 1870 and 1920, the American dream was not just a compelling ideal but a last chance at survival. Many found work building skyscrapers, bridges, subways, and trolley lines in the growing cities. The skyscraper itself was an icon of high hopes and upward mobility. It became the most visible symbol of America's confidence although, ironically, the many "invisible" immigrants who built them seldom gained appreciation or recognition. To whom did these magnificent buildings truly belong, the people who built them or the people who owned them? In his play *The Hairy Ape*, Eugene O'Neill captured the anguish experienced by workers who identified with the symbols of economic power even as they themselves remained poor:

> Yuh don't belong, get me! Look at me, why don't youse dare? I belong, dat's me! (*pointing to a skyscraper across the street which is in the process of contruction—with bravado*). See dat building goin' up dere? See de steel work? Steel, dat's me! Youse guys live on it and tink yuh're sumep'n. But I'm in it, see! Sure! I'm steel and steam and smoke and de rest of it! It moves—speed—twenty-five stories up—and me at de top and bottom—movin'! Youse simps don't move. Yuh're on'y dolls I winds up to see 'm spin.

After the passage of the restrictive quota laws, the great waves of immigrants from Europe subsided during the 1920s as well as during the Great Depression of the 1930s. Still, the United States continued to be a "land of opportunity" for those in need. In the 1960s, quotas based on nationality were lifted, and another wave of immigrants came mainly from Asia and the West Indies rather than from Europe.

These new immigrants came for the same reason as their predecessors a century before: to make a better life for themselves and their families.

The tallest building in the world when it opened in 1913, the Woolworth Building in New York City was a masterpiece of engineering technology and neogothic architecture.

∽ **Notes**

_____

_____

_____

_____

_____

_____

_____

_____

Technological Progress in a Progressive Era

Sleek and modern, the Empire State Building heralded the new modern age with its rise to the sky in a series of setbacks (step-like building elements), topped with a pointed spire. It symbolized the belief in progress inherent in the American Dream. At 102 stories high, it stood for decades as the tallest building in the world. Completed in 1931, this building became an icon of America's confidence about its rightful place at the top. The Empire State Building owed its existence, its urban location, and its inspiration to a number of inventions that came from the Progressive Era: the metal building-frame and the safety elevator; the telegraph and telephone; the railroad, the car, and the airplane.

Building Trades: the Metal Frame and Safety Elevator

What is the definition of a skyscraper? Who built the first skyscraper? And when? Architects endlessly debate these questions. Some define a skyscraper as any building so tall that residents cannot easily climb stairs to reach the top. Others define a skyscraper as a tall building with a metal frame.

As buildings got taller and taller, their walls got thicker and thicker, the thicker walls being necessary to carry the extra weight. At a certain point additional height proved impractical because the thick walls took up too much space and made the interior of the building too dark. Traditional buildings with load-bearing walls could usually reach only 10 or 11 stories. Once architects perfected the metal frame, buildings could be built much higher than before. The strong metal frame, not the walls, carried the weight of the building.

The metal frame was not so much invented as perfected and refined from cast iron building components, which had been first manufactured in England in the 18th century. Necessity—including

One of the first "artistic" skyscrapers, the 21-story Fuller Building, built in New York City in 1902, became instantly known as the "Flatiron Building" due to its unusual shape. The aerodynamic shape of the Flatiron Building created a wind tunnel effect at the intersection of 23rd Street and Fifth Avenue, where crowds of men would gather to catch a titillating glimpse of a lady's bare ankle as the winds lifted her skirt. The phrase "23 skidoo," which now means simply to leave quickly, originated among New York City policemen as a codeword for dispersing the gawking crowd at the Flatiron Building.

the need for stronger bridges, expansive factory work floors, and taller buildings—urged on this process of refinement. Many architects and engineers consider the Home Insurance Building that was completed in 1885 the first skyscraper. Built in Chicago by William LeBaron Jenney, it stood 10 stories tall with most of its weight resting on its metal frame.

Tall skyscrapers would have been useless if safe elevators had not been developed to transport occupants to the upper floors. Similar to the development of metal frames, safe elevators were not so much invented as perfected. Simple pulleys had been used since prehistoric times. The ancient Greeks had devised simple elevators to help carry loads. It was not until the 1850s, however, that Elisha G. Otis manufactured relatively safe steam and hydraulic passenger elevators. Electricity (whose application to light bulbs brightened the Progressive Era) began to power elevators in 1889.

Communication: Telegraph and Telephone

While the building trades offered inventions that made skyscrapers technically feasible, the communication and transportation industries made them desirable. Telegraph lines crossed the continent in the 1850s, soon being matched by telephone lines in the 1880s. Telegraphs and telephones allowed factory bosses to keep in touch with their factories while working at another location. Many supervisors and owners preferred to work in a central downtown district close to other supervisors, other business owners, bankers, stockbrokers, and clerical staff. As more and more businesses established offices "downtown," land values in central downtown districts soared, making it more economical to build very tall buildings on relatively small lots of land.

Transportation: Trains, Cars, and Airplanes

By the 1850s, trains began to transport not only shoppers and tourists into the cities but also migrating farmers. This contributed to the transformation of America from a rural to an urban society. To accommodate the shoppers and tourists, restaurants,

∼ Notes

Use a cluster diagram to examine how inventions facilitated the growth of the city.

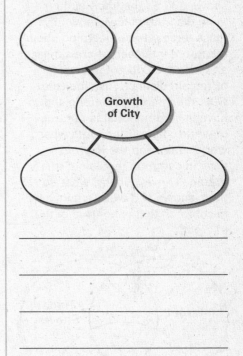

Notes

In 1893 people learned about new trends at world's fairs. Today we can learn about new trends at trade shows and on the Internet. In the Venn diagram below, show how these three ways of learning about the future intersect, or are similar, and how they do not intersect, or remain distinct. Also indicate what the Internet and trade shows have in common that is not true of world's fairs. Then, note what world's fairs and the Internet have in common that is not true of trade shows. Finally, what do trade shows and world's fairs have in common that is not true of the Internet.

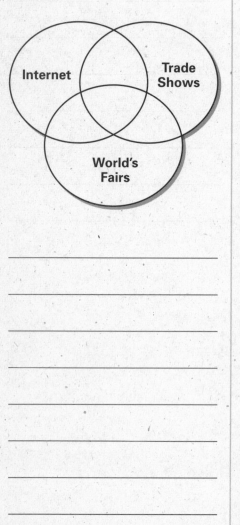

_____

_____

_____

_____

_____

_____

_____

entertainment palaces, athletic clubs, and department stores sprang up. By 1904, New York boasted of a subway system. Employed laborers ran steam and electric streetcars, elevated trains, and cable cars as they transported ever more workers into the central city. Henry Ford founded the Ford Motor Company in 1903. Soon he was providing affordable mass-produced cars to the middle class and making longer commutes possible.

Transportation, including engine-powered airplanes (first flown by the Wright brothers in 1903), not only transported, but also inspired. The Progressive Era, as its name implies, rejoiced in technical progress. Art Deco, a style of decorative and industrial arts of the 1920s, celebrated progress in its modern forms of transportation. In architecture, Art Deco setbacks, fluted columns, and zigzag aluminum decoration suggested the dramatic movement and speed of modern transport vehicles. The sleek buildings imitated the aerodynamic designs of fast trains and planes. The Empire State Building embodied and perfected the Art Deco aesthetic, its upward thrust paralleling the upward mobility that the American Dream promised.

World's Fairs

During the 19th century, world's fairs became important places for learning about science and technology as well as a way to satisfy shoppers' curiosity about new consumer products. It may have been at the first World's Fair in England in 1851 that a metal-frame and glass exhibit hall, called the Crystal Palace, inspired engineers to dream about metal-frame skyscrapers.

By 1893, when the World's Columbian Exposition set up in Chicago, the skyscraper had already been invented. Not only that, skyscrapers were flourishing, with buildings 12 and 16 stories tall and soon even taller. From a distance, the skyscrapers of Chicago's "Loop" could be seen from the fairgrounds south of the city where visitors strolled along promenades and viewed dazzling displays of modern electric inventions. One of the most whimsical inventions at the Columbian Exposition was an electric Ferris wheel 250 feet in diameter. Nighttime crowds waited in line to take a ride as they watched the bright electric light bulbs circling the giant wheel. Throughout the grounds, an eerie illumination, often punctuated by a show of exploding fireworks, seemed to create a "sudden vision of heaven," one visitor exclaimed.

∿ **Notes**

The Role of African Americans

Tourists nicknamed the 1893 fairgrounds "the white city." The name referred to the serene white buildings and fountains that stood on the grounds. To journalist Ida B. Wells, however, the name had other connotations. Although the fair had exhibits from Africa and had scheduled a "colored day" on which African Americans could organize and attend, African American people were not allowed to participate on an equal basis. Wells called for a boycott of "colored day" and wrote the pamphlet "The Reason Why the Colored American Is Not in the World's Columbian Exposition." The following letter by W. J. Crawford, an African American who had applied to be a guard at the fair, appeared in Wells's pamphlet. Crawford never received a reply to his letter addressed to the Board of Control of the Fair.

PRIMARY SOURCE: LETTER

from *Letter to the Board of Control of the Fair*
March 15, 1893

Dear Sir:

. . . on the first day of March, 1893, I made a formal application and was subjected to the required examination by the medical examiner. At the conclusion of my examination, I was told by the examining surgeon that I had met every requirement and was in every way qualified except in the single point of chest measurement; the rule of the department requires a chest measurement of thirty-six inches, but the said medical examiner stated in his certificate of examination that my chest measurement was less than thirty-five inches, and further marked on said certificate the gratuitous information "not rejected on account of color."

I appeal to your honorable board for a reopening of my application for appointment as a Columbian Guard on the following grounds:

I am satisfied that my application was rejected solely on account of my color. . . . I went to no less eminent physician than Dr. S. N. Davis of this city. [T]he finding of Dr. Davis's examination is in direct contradiction to the alleged measurement of the medical examiner. . . . It is a significant fact that every colored applicant, thus far, has been rejected for causes more or less trivial, or, as in my case, false. . . .

Obediently yours,
W. J. Crawford
No. 400 27th street

∿ END ∿

_____

_____

_____

_____

_____

_____

_____

Young doffer boy at machine in Lindale, Georgia, in April 1913.

The Dark Side of the American Dream

When tourists visited the world's fairs in Chicago and then in St. Louis at the turn of the last century, many brought with them a Kodak camera, an inexpensive box camera that first came out in the 1880s. While amateurs took shots of family and friends in carefree, happy poses at the fairs, photographer Lewis Hine carried a heavy tripod to other places in the United States to document the dark side of the American Dream, the world of sweatshop families and child laborers. As a teacher, Hine had used the camera only as a pedagogical device, to capture the interest of his young students. He planned field trips (1905) to Ellis Island and, with his students, snapped photos of immigrants as they went through processing at the immigration center. Drawn to the place, Hine returned again and again, but soon his purpose for doing so was not pedagogical but photographic. He had found his true calling as a social-activist photographer.

On Ellis Island, Hine approached his immigrant subjects with respect and decorum, communicating with smiles and gestures, for he did not know their languages. He gained their friendship and trust as he sought to capture on film the essence of their lives. Conditions were far from ideal, but Hine persevered, goaded by his desire to document the hidden truths of his own era. He followed his subjects into the city and witnessed their hardships there. He climbed the many staircases of the tenement houses, feeling he might find his most poignant photograph of sweatshop conditions on the very top floor.

In 1910 Hine boarded a train, hired by the National Child Labor Committee to travel and document child labor in the United States. He visited coal mines in Pennsylvania, cigar factories in Florida, glass shops in West Virginia, and cotton textile mills in Georgia.

The textile factories offer a typical example of what life as laborers meant for children. Children often started out as helpers. Their parents, poor whites from mountain areas, had come to mill towns to find work. Since mill towns seldom built schools, the children accompanied their parents to work when they were still toddlers. In this way, they learned their future jobs. Some began working in earnest by the time they were only six or seven, though theoretically regulations forbade a child to work before the age of twelve.

In the mills, Hine photographed young doffers—boys who had to change bobbins or mend broken thread. Some were so short that they had to climb up on the frame of the dangerous machine to reach the bobbin—and often without shoes. Being poor they had no choice. Some lost toes or fingers. Most of the boys smoked cigarettes. World weary, old beyond their years, they toiled for 10 to 12 hours a day for dimes. Hine asked the subject of his photo "Baby Doffer" how old he was. The small boy hesitated and then said, "I'm twelve." Another young boy immediately confided, "He can't work unless he's twelve."

While the conditions for such working youth were improving through the efforts of various social reform movements, the realization of the American Dream was hardly within their grasp. The arrival of the new century, however, held the hope of the unknown, and immigrants, like African Americans, continued their struggle to establish an identity within the American social landscape.

~ Notes

_____

_____

_____

_____

_____

(Top:) Doffer boys in Bibb Mill #1 in Macon, Georgia, in January 1909.

(Bottom:) Seven-year-old sweeper and twelve-year-old doffer boy in Roanoke, Virginia, in May 1911.

The Modern Age

EVENTS IN AMERICAN LITERATURE

1910   **1920**

1912 Harriet Monroe founds *Poetry* magazine, which would introduce many modernist poets

1915 Early poem by T. S. Eliot, "The Love Song of J. Alfred Prufrock," first appears in *Poetry*

1916 Robert Frost's "The Road Not Taken" is published

1917 The first collection of *The Cantos* by Ezra Pound is published in *Poetry*

1919 Claude McKay writes "If We Must Die" during summer wave of violence against African Americans

1920s Harlem Renaissance is in its heyday

1922 Groundbreaking anthology, *The Book of American Negro Poetry*, is compiled by James Weldon Johnson

1925 Countee Cullen publishes his first book of poetry, *Color*

EVENTS IN NORTH AMERICA

1910   **1920**

1896 Supreme Court rules "separate but equal" is constitutional in *Plessy v. Ferguson*

1909 Sixty prominent black and white citizens found National Association for the Advancement of Colored People (NAACP) to end discrimination and prevent violence against black people

1910 Dixieland jazz arises in New Orleans

1913 Armory Show in New York City exhibits modern art to large crowds and horrified critics

1915 Ku Klux Klan revitalized in Georgia, then nationwide

1916–1919 Great Migration of African Americans from the South to northern cities

1917 United States enters World War I, ensuring the Allied victory a year later

1918–1921 Red Scare in United States

1919 Congress ratifies 18th Amendment, which prohibits manufacture, transportation, and sale of alcoholic beverages, ushering in Prohibition

1919–1921 Palmer Raids against dissidents, anarchists, and Communist sympathizers in the United States; many immigrants arrested and deported

1920s Decade called the Roaring Twenties; symbolized by the freewheeling flappers

1920s Huge availability and popularity of the radio

1920 U.S. Bureau of Census reports that for the first time the nation's rural population is less than half of total population

1921 First radio coverage of World Series demonstrates radio's growing popularity

EVENTS IN THE WORLD

1910   **1920**

1912 Qing Dynasty, in power in China since 1644, is overthrown by nationalist revolt in favor of a republic

1914 War erupts in Europe between Central Powers (Germany and Austria-Hungary) and Allies (Great Britain, France, and Russia)

1914 World War I begins in Europe, ends 1918

1917 United States enters World War I

1917 V. I. Lenin leads Bolshevik Revolution that topples Russian czar

1918 The Allies, with U.S. help, defeat Central Powers, ending World War I; Bolsheviks become Russian Communist Party

1919 The Treaty of Versailles is signed by Allies and Associated Powers and by Germany

1920 Hitler takes control of new National Socialist German Workers' (Nazi) Party

1921 Mao Zedong co-founds China's Communist Party

1930

1925 Alain Locke publishes "Enter the New Negro"

1926 Langston Hughes publishes *The Weary Blues*, depicting life in Harlem in the 1920s; Ernest Hemingway publishes his first novel, *The Sun Also Rises*

1928 Zora Neale Hurston publishes "How It Feels to Be Colored Me"

1930 Katherine Anne Porter's "The Jilting of Granny Weatherall" appears in collection titled *Flowering Judas*

1931 Arna Bontemps's first novel, *God Sends Sunday*, is published

1933 Gertrude Stein publishes The Autobiography of *Alice B. Toklas*

1934 Dorothy West founds *Challenge*, a literary magazine for African American writers

1936 Dorothy Parker publishes *Collected Poems: Not So Deep as a Well*

1939 John Steinbeck writes *The Grapes of Wrath*, depicting the plight of farmers ruined by the Depression and the Dust Bowl

1930

1922 Louis Armstrong joins King Oliver's Creole Jazz Band in Chicago, heralding Jazz Age

1923 Performance of the Charleston in musical *Runnin' Wild* starts nationwide dance craze

1924 Congress passes the Federal Road Act, and highways are built across America to accommodate growing number of automobiles

1927 Charles Lindbergh is first to fly solo across Atlantic, nonstop from New York to Paris; Babe Ruth hits season record of 60 home runs (since surpassed); first "talking" movie, *The Jazz Singer,* is released

1929 Stock-market crash on Wall Street plunges nation into Great Depression

1930 Great Depression hits the nation

1931 Empire State Building is completed, the world's then-tallest building at 102 stories

1932 Franklin Delano Roosevelt is elected president at height of Depression, with nearly one-third of work force unemployed

1934–1936 Dust Bowl in the Great Plains

1938 Congress passes Fair Labor Standards Act, which establishes minimum wage and provides for adoption of 40-hour workweek

1939 First regular television broadcasts begin

1930

1928 Joseph Stalin becomes dictator of Communist Russia

1930 Nationalists and Communists fight civil war in China

1932 Saudi Arabia declares itself a single kingdom

1933 Hitler and Nazis seize dictatorial control of Germany

1937 Japan invades China

1938 English prime minister claims "peace in our time" after ceding parts of Czechoslovakia to Hitler

1939 Germany invades Poland and World War II begins

∼ Notes

_____

_____

_____

_____

_____

_____

_____

_____

_____

_____

_____

_____

_____

_____

_____

_____

_____

_____

A New Cultural Identity: The Harlem Renaissance

In the 1920s, Harlem, a section of northern Manhattan in New York City, became a center of world-class African American art, music, and literature. Harlem was a magnet that drew thousands of blacks who migrated north from the South and Midwest, fleeing Jim Crow discrimination and Klan violence. Among these newcomers were some of the most talented African Americans our country has ever produced. Harlem became a vibrant cultural mecca, whose art, philosophy, literature, and music gave rise to African Americans' cultural identity.

The philosopher Alain Locke gave voice to the new confidence of Harlem when he rejected the era's demeaning treatment and stereotypes of blacks. In his essay "Enter the New Negro" he urged African Americans to define themselves in their own way, celebrating their abilities and their culture and recognizing that all blacks were one people with a common heritage. Marcus Garvey was a more radical champion of the uniqueness of African American culture. He wrote extensively, urging blacks to turn their backs on an America that repressed them and return to their roots in Africa. Garvey's back-to-Africa movement was founded on black pride and his belief that African Americans should develop their own society and culture and turn their backs on a white culture that would never accept or value them.

The intellectuals, artists, and writers of the Harlem Renaissance embodied the liberated spirit of Locke's New Negro. Langston Hughes, one of America's greatest poets, praised blackness and black culture in his many volumes of poetry. Zora Neale Hurston's novels, short stories, and essays reveal her love of African American traditions, language, and manners. She was one of the first writers to write about African Americans, not as stereotypes, but as complete, complex, and multifaceted human beings.

African American music had been evolving since blacks were first transported to this country from Africa. By the 1920s, the blues was a well-established musical form. As the black experience became more urbanized, a unique and quintessentially African American music arose—jazz. Like the blues, jazz gave a musical voice to the African American experience. Many people around the world consider jazz to be America's greatest and most unique contribution to world culture.

Harlem in the first decades of the 20th century thrummed and swayed to the sounds of jazz. Duke Ellington, Louis Armstrong, and numerous other jazz musicians flocked to Harlem to play the extraordinary and innovative music at clubs around the neighborhood and in other parts of the city.

As with so many other aspects of African American life at the time, most jazz clubs were segregated, and blacks and whites could not enjoy the music together. Segregation was a fact of life for blacks then. Earlier, African American men who had joined the Armed Forces to fight in World War I served in segregated units and were not allowed to fight. Though the Ku Klux Klan was not as active and violent up north as in other areas, Jim Crow laws and inherent racism, which restricted blacks' access to public services and civil rights, were commonplace throughout the nation.

The terrible discrimination suffered by African Americans in the South at the time was a major impetus for them to rediscover and reinvent themselves as a people. By relocating to Harlem and other cities in the North, many African Americans distanced themselves from the prevailing racial attitudes of white Americans in the twenties, and energized the rebirth of a distinct and vibrant African American culture.

~ Notes

_____

_____

_____

_____

_____

_____

_____

_____

_____

_____

Duke Ellington and his orchestra, shown here performing at the Hurricane Club in New York City, played a significant role in the development of jazz. The prolific band recorded an estimated 2,000 musical compositions, ranging from popular songs and comedies to film scores and an opera.

_____

_____

_____

_____

_____

_____

_____

_____

_____

_____

Jim Crow, the Klan, and the Great Migration

The end of the Civil War in 1865 officially ended the institution of slavery in the South and freed the nation's African Americans. But Southerners feared that the newly freed blacks would overwhelm white culture, or even seek revenge. To preserve their dominance, southerners legislated strict separation of the races through the Black Codes, laws that essentially perpetuated the prewar exclusion of blacks from southern life. In 1896, the U.S. Supreme Court ruled, in *Plessy* v. *Ferguson,* that "separate but equal" facilities and social institutions were not a violation of blacks' constitutional rights. This decision led to a deluge of statutes codifying segregation through Jim Crow laws. (The term Jim Crow supposedly arose from a white minstrel show performer who blackened his face with charcoal, danced a jig, and sang the song "Jump Jim Crow." By the 1850s, the Jim Crow character had become a stereotype of alleged black inferiority.)

Beginning in the 1890s, Jim Crow laws began segregating or excluding blacks from virtually every aspect of southern public life. The intent was to prevent all contact between the races. The fundamental principle was that any white person was superior to any black person and any black person was inferior to any white person. For this system to work, there could be no exceptions; any whites or blacks who flouted the laws risked economic or physical "correction."

Where practical, Jim Crow laws enforced segregation. African Americans were segregated from whites in most public spaces, including schools, parks, and transportation. Where blacks were allowed to share certain public facilities, such as theaters or bus waiting rooms, they entered through separate doors and occupied strictly separate areas. On city buses, blacks and whites lined up separately. Whites entered first at the front. Blacks paid at the front but entered via the back door to ensure that they did not touch a

Segregated drinking fountains were just one of the many restrictions African Americans lived with under Jim Crow laws. The institutionalized racism impacted all areas of life, with separate schools, separate textbooks, separate railroad cars, and even separate burial grounds.

white passenger as they walked down the aisle to their rear seats. If separation was impractical, exclusion was enforced. In many southern states, blacks were excluded from libraries, hotels, and public swimming pools. In Oklahoma, the phone company was required to provide separate phones for blacks after whites refused to use public phones that had been handled by African Americans. In Alabama, among other states, blacks were legally bound to observe a curfew to keep them off the streets after dark. Numerous laws prevented blacks from voting by setting up black-only poll taxes, literacy tests, or other obstacles that disenfranchised African Americans.

After Emancipation, many powerful southerners made it clear that black lives were worth little. Jim Crow laws were often enforced with brutal violence; sometimes, a black man or woman was beaten or killed not for any infraction but as a reminder to other blacks that whites held power and could use it with impunity.

Surviving the terror of Jim Crow forced blacks to live "behind the veil" in a form of "double-consciousness," in W. E. B. DuBois's words. In public, blacks assumed a non-confrontational mask to project acceptance of their inferior status and hide their true feelings of rage and humiliation. "Putting on the face" showed ostensible conformation to the "racial etiquette" that was required for survival, but it took an enormous psychological toll on African Americans. Blacks avoided looking at whites (they were to stare at the ground when being spoken to); black men, especially, were forbidden to make eye contact with white women. Infractions would cost blacks, at the least, their jobs, homes or farm tenancies, and their ability to buy supplies in white-owned businesses. At the worst, they'd be beaten or lynched.

The term *lynching* means murder by a mob, or execution without due process of law. Often, lynchings followed a real or imagined transgression against racial laws or etiquette. Sometimes, it was used randomly as an object lesson or simply as a form of spectator

∼ Notes

Use a cluster diagram to examine various aspects of Jim Crow laws.

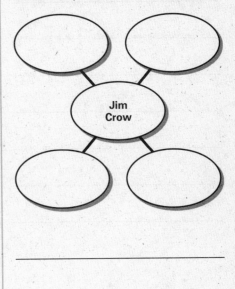

_____

_____

_____

_____

_____

_____

_____

_____

_____

_____

_____

_____

_____

_____

_____

_____

_____

_____

_____

_____

_____

_____

_____

_____

_____

_____

_____

_____

_____

_____

_____

"sport." Lynchings usually entailed hanging from a tree, but sometimes involved burning, dragging behind a vehicle, shooting, knifing, or beating. Between 1880 and 1950, at least 5,000 men and women were lynched by the Ku Klux Klan.

In 1915, outside Stone Mountain, Georgia, the Klan, a moribund organization left over from Reconstruction, gained new life with the release of D.W. Griffith's film *Birth of a Nation*. By the mid-1920s, the Klan boasted 4 million members nationwide—and not only in the South. It was a terrorist organization that firmly believed that the separation of the races was "decreed by the Creator." Klansmen would commit any atrocity to keep blacks in a state of permanent debasement. Many respected citizens, including members of Congress (who repeatedly defeated anti-lynching bills), were members. Lynching and organized terror were the Klan's specialties and came to be an accepted part of the social fabric from Indiana to Florida.

It is easy to see why blacks were desperate to leave the South. In the 1880s and 1890s, thousands left to settle in Kansas and Oklahoma, where they hoped to create black-only towns and be left in peace. Thousands of sharecroppers moved to southern cities, such as Atlanta, to escape terror and crushing rural poverty. After black enlisted men returned home after World War I they were less inclined to tolerate the inferior status imposed on them by Jim Crow. These men led an exodus from the South. Between 1916 and 1919—the period of the Great Migration—more than half a million blacks moved north to large cities, such as Chicago, Detroit, and New York. During the 1920s, another million took the road north. Many of the migrants followed relatives or friends who had moved north earlier to take jobs in military industries.

Many African Americans gravitated to Harlem. Earlier migrants had found good jobs in New York. This large black population attracted black professionals to Harlem, where they became prosperous. Many African American intellectuals— W. E. B. DuBois and Marcus Garvey among them—were centered in Harlem. Many black intellectuals admired DuBois's ideas about improving the conditions of blacks and restoring black pride and a new black identity. Garvey had founded the Universal Negro Improvement Association, which held conventions in New York. Many talented and intellectual African Americans came to the city to attend these conventions, and many stayed to contribute to the Harlem Renaissance.

PRIMARY SOURCE: ESSAY

Enter the New Negro
by Alain Locke

In the last decade something beyond the watch and guard of statistics has happened in the life of the American Negro. . . . For the younger generation is vibrant with a new psychology; the new spirit is awake in the masses . . . transforming what has been a perennial problem into the progressive phases of contemporary Negro life . . .

. . . [F]or generations in the mind of America, the Negro has been more of a formula than a human being—a something to be argued . . . or worried over, harassed, or patronized, a social bogey or a social burden. . . .

Recall how suddenly the Negro spirituals revealed themselves; suppressed for generations . . . secretive, half-ashamed, until the courage of being natural brought them out . . . Similarly the mind of the Negro seems suddenly to have slipped from under the tyranny of social intimidation and to be shaking off the psychology of imitation and implied inferiority. By shedding the old chrysalis of the Negro problem we are achieving something like a spiritual emancipation. . . .

With this renewed self-respect and self-dependence, the life of the Negro community is bound to enter a new dynamic phase, the buoyancy from within compensating for whatever pressure there may be of conditions from without.

continued on page 132

⌒ Notes

Take notes on the selection using a cluster diagram to organize the most important information about what the New Negro is and what he or she must do to become the type of person Locke describes.

the New Negro

. . . [The] Young Negro, in his poetry, his art, his education, and his new outlook . . . [has] the poise and greater certainty of knowing what it is all about. From this comes the promise and warrant of a new leadership. As one of them has discerningly put it:

> We have tomorrow
> Bright before us
> Like a flame.
> Yesterday, a night-gone thing
> A sun-down name.
>
> And dawn today
> Broad arch above the road we came.
> We march!

This is what . . . requires that the Negro of today be seen through other than the dusty spectacles of past controversy.

The Negro, too, . . . has idols . . . to smash. If on the one hand the white man has erred in making the Negro appear to be that which would excuse or extenuate his treatment of him, the Negro, in turn, has too often unnecessarily excused himself because of the way he has been treated. The intelligent Negro of today is resolved not to make discrimination an extenuation for his shortcomings in performance, individual or collective . . . For this he must know himself and be known for precisely what he is, . . .

. . . [T]here are constructive channels opening out into which the balked social feelings of the American Negro can flow freely. . . . These compensating interests are racial but in a new and enlarged way. One is the consciousness of acting as the advance-guard of the African peoples in their contact with Twentieth Century civilization . . . Harlem, as we shall see, is the center of these movements; she is the home of the Negro's "Zionism." The pulse of the Negro world has begun to beat in Harlem.

from *Survey Graphic: Harlem, Mecca of the New Negro,* March 1925

~ END ~

Music of the Harlem Renaissance

A Brief History of African American Music

African Americans brought their music with them from West Africa, and they eased their forced labor with song. The most common West African singing was the call-and-response, in which one person sings a lyric and others repeat it. In the South, work songs and field hollers were improvised for every type of labor, and music was integral to spiritual survival. Shouts were energetic, uplifting songs of praise sung by large groups and usually accompanied by rhythmic clapping and stomping in circle dances. Sometimes called "ring spirituals," shouts were expressions of religious fervor.

Many whites found the texture of black music complex and unlike the musical forms with which they were familiar. Though ostensibly everyone sang the same melody, none were identical. Each singer expressed individual feeling, using grace notes and slurs, their voices ranging above and below the notes of the melody. Most scholars today call this *heterophony*, in which singers follow the lead but wander from the melody at will. Singers also used a variety of styles: recitative, yelling, moaning, growling, and falsetto. Melodic improvisation was always a key element in African American music.

The most common musical instruments were the fiddle and banjo (drums were prohibited—their association with Africa scared whites). Several different rhythms were kept simultaneously by clapping or stomping. The music was multi-rhythmic, or *syncopated*, with emphases on different beats.

The themes of antebellum black music often invoked the longing "to go home," to be free of life's tribulations. The will to "overcome" oppression, an optimism that faith will redeem one's suffering, and a joy in final release were common themes, as were expressions of feeling about daily life and shared or individual hardship.

∿ Notes

Compare the styles of music of early, enslaved African Americans, of the blues, and of jazz using a chart like the one below.

African American	Blues	Jazz

_____

_____

_____

_____

PRIMARY SOURCE: BLUES LYRICS

Ramblin' On My Mind
by Robert Johnson

I got ramblin'
    I got ramblin' on my mind
I got ramblin'
    I got ramblin' on my mind
Hate to leave you my baby
    but you treat me so unkind
I got mean things
    I got mean things on my mind
Little girl, Little girl
    I got mean things on my mind
Hate to leave you here babe
    but you treat me so unkind
Runnin' down to the station
    catch the first mail train I see
Runnin' down to the station
    catch that old first mail train I see
I got the blues 'bout Miss So and So
    and the child got the blues 'bout me
And I'm leavin' this morning
    with my arm fold up and cryin'
And I'm leavin' this morning
    with my arm fold up and cryin'
I hate to leave my baby
    but she treats me so unkind
I got mean things
    I got mean things on my mind
I got mean things
    I got mean things on my mind
I got to leave my baby
    'cause she treats me so unkind

~ END ~

It isn't hard to see how the blues grew out of this music. Both use slurring and bending of notes and different oral styles, though blues themes are usually personal and may contain irony and humor. Most blues players use the guitar (an instrument rooted in Arab culture) instead of the banjo (an instrument rooted in African culture). Yet despite clear parallels between the blues and early black music, no one knows how the blues started or was named. W. C. Handy, the "father of the blues," reports first hearing the blues at a train station in Tutwiler, Mississippi in 1903, where he encountered "a lean, loose-jointed Negro plunking a guitar."

The song he sang, Handy says, "struck me instantly." Ma Rainey, a queen of blues singing, claimed to have heard the blues in 1902 in Missouri. It is likely that the blues was a logical evolution from antebellum black music and that no one ever really "invented" the form. Robert Johnson, perhaps the greatest blues singer and acoustic guitarist of all time, lived and played in the Mississippi Delta in the twenties.

The blues are played in a "blues scale," in which some notes are bent and lowered a half step to produce a "blue note," or minor-key sound. Many blues melodies have been traced to the cadences of hollers. The blues form contains several three-line verses in which the first line is repeated once, followed by a different lyric. The lyrics are intensely personal and often sexual, describing feelings of loss, desire, loneliness, and betrayal.

Though the blues influenced jazz, it is most likely that jazz arose via another evolutionary line. The earliest jazz form arose around 1910 in New Orleans, home of Dixieland jazz, an irresistibly buoyant and joyous music. A typical Dixieland band had five to seven musicians, who played brass, bass, piano, and sometimes banjo. All instruments played together, and improvisation was the specialty of soloists—most notably Louis Armstrong, who began his career in King Oliver's band.

In the 1920s, true jazz emerged in Chicago as a unique musical form. The era's big bands, with 15 to 20 musicians, played sophisticated musical arrangements. Though the emphasis was on ensemble playing, soloists were exemplary improvisers. The typical big band had four sections: saxophones, trumpets, trombones, and rhythm (piano, drums, guitar, bass).

What exactly is jazz? Many describe it as a conversation, a call-and-response, among instruments. Musicians improvise based on their knowledge of and feeling for the music. Jazz often uses widely recognized songs and complex patterns of rhythm, syncopation, and improvised chord changes in the melody, traits traceable to early African American music.

The twenties were the Jazz Age. Fletcher Henderson led one of the era's most popular jazz bands. Duke Ellington and his big band were the toast of Harlem, playing the Cotton Club for 11 years. As a bandleader and composer, Ellington wrote and performed hundreds of jazz classics. Ellington's bands were known for their collective improvisation and stellar soloists. His swinging sound gave rise to the big-band sound of the 1930s Swing Era.

The worldwide popularity of jazz was fostered by Edison's invention of the phonograph and the burgeoning new record industry. Jumpin' big-band dance music could be heard and played not only in Harlem, but also in dancehalls and living rooms around the country.

Copyright © McDougal Littell Inc.

∿ Notes

Much of the fighting of World War I took place in the trenches, long narrow ditches where soldiers lived and fought, out of the line of enemy fire. Trenches ranged from 6 to 8 feet deep, and would often fill with water from rain. Rat infestation, body lice, trench foot and shell shock were the scourge of trench life.

~ Notes

_____

_____

_____

_____

_____

_____

_____

_____

_____

_____

_____

_____

Alienation of the Individual: Modernism

World War I devastated Europe, bringing death and disillusionment to the people of the 32 nations involved. It was the first large-scale modern war to use savage technological weapons, such as poison gas and machine guns. By the war's end in 1918, about 10 million soldiers and an equal number of civilians had died. The United States entered the war in 1917 and shared Europe's sense that civilization as people had known it had been ineffaceably altered. The trauma of war and the political breakdown that ensued left many thoughtful people anxious and uncertain. Many ordinary Americans became more fearful of foreigners and intolerant of political dissent. Idealism was thrown into question though economic prosperity and technology grew. Many people, tired of war, just wanted to have fun. During the Roaring Twenties, some Americans had more money than they ever had. Instead of saving it, as previous generations might have done, they spent it on good times. People bought the newly available radios and cars. They went to nightclubs and dancehalls. Jazz music and moving pictures became popular entertainment.

The Roaring Twenties were also rampant with political corruption and gangsterism, primarily a result of the Volstead Act of 1919, which prohibited the manufacture and sale of intoxicating beverages. While social reformers had looked to prohibition as a panacea for such societal ills as unemployment, domestic violence, poverty, and crime, no one foresaw its potential as an unlimited source of corruption, greed, and violence. According to critics, prohibition not only failed to decrease the use of alcohol, but actually served to popularize drinking among youth, promote consumption of hard alcohol over beer, and encourage corruption at all levels of government. Criminal gangs organized to profit from the lucrative business of bootlegging and smuggling of alcohol. In 1927, Al Capone reportedly made 60 million dollars from bootlegging and had half of the Chicago police force on his payroll.

Gangland violence became increasingly commonplace, as did arrests for drunkenness and disorderly conduct, drunk driving, theft, burglary, and assault and battery. Federal spending on prisons increased more than 1,000 percent between 1915 and 1932. The most serious indictment of prohibition came when the Act was repealed and crime rates dropped drastically and immediately.

But the unease experienced by many Americans in the face of the new level of crime, violence and corruption did not dissipate as rapidly, and further compounded the atmosphere of anxiety in the wake of World War I.

Modernism was a literary movement that arose in response to these social and cultural conditions. The most prestigious writing expressed disillusionment with the era's materialism and hypocrisy. Every modernist writer, including Gertrude Stein, James Joyce, and T. S. Eliot had a distinct style. Yet they shared certain characteristics, including their conviction that individuals were becoming increasingly threatened by mass society. Modernist characters nearly always embodied this alienation, typically being withdrawn, unresponsive, and in psychic pain caused by a combination of social forces. Another characteristic common to modernist writers was their drive to experiment with new forms of writing. Some used stream-of-consciousness techniques to show the thoughts of their characters; others wrote short, choppy sentences to express the fragmentation of the modern character's experience. Modernists are also as noted for what they leave out of their writing as for what they put in. Writers omitted narrative and explanation, putting the reader in the sometimes challenging position of having to figure out what is going on in a story or poem and what a character or speaker is truly feeling or thinking.

The concerns of modernism dominated the arts and literature throughout the 20th century. Great plays of the time—especially Tennessee Williams's *A Streetcar Named Desire* (1951) and Arthur Miller's *Death of a Salesman* (1949)—feature characters trapped by their own flaws and thoughtlessly pushed aside and destroyed by the brutal forces of society. Women's poems of the era often expressed bitterness and anger at the pressures women of the time were under to conform to societal norms.

~ **Notes**

_____

_____

_____

_____

_____

_____

_____

_____

_____

_____

_____

_____

_____

_____

_____

_____

_____

_____

_____

Socialism in the United States and the Red Scare

"Woe to the man . . . that seeks to stand in our way in this day of high resolution," stated President Woodrow Wilson after he committed the United States to fight in World War I. The government's total commitment to war prepared fertile ground for the fears and irrational hatreds simmering in America at that time. Blind hatred of foreigners and "foreign" ideas—especially those from Germany—was encouraged. Propaganda, censorship, and hatemongering proliferated.

By 1918, the Communist revolution in Russia was well underway. Communism was the perfect target for the violent and hateful emotions that led to the nationwide Red Scare. The media blared warnings against the Communist hordes and urged citizens to be vigilant against anything even remotely "red." Soon, any criticism of the government or American life was considered treasonous.

At this same time, millions of immigrants from Eastern and Southern Europe were entering the country, seeking work and citizenship. Many impoverished immigrants took what work they could get, laboring in the worst of conditions, earning starvation wages. The IWW (Industrial Workers of the World), or Wobblies, tried to unionize both native-born and immigrant workers. In Europe, the example of Russia was energizing a strong labor movement, even giving rise to Communist parties. The IWW was an obvious target for U.S. hatemongers and anti-Communists. Wobblies were beaten, jailed, and even killed for trying to organize workers. Any criticism of the United States was a crime under the Alien and Sedition Acts, and punished by jail time. Some outspoken critics were lynched. Union organizers, anarchists, socialists, pacifists, and others who dared exercise their First Amendment rights were persecuted or prosecuted.

The situation worsened when out-of-control inflation raged in 1919, with the dollar losing half its purchasing power. Workers, already unfairly exploited, suffered real privation. Thousands marched in the streets. A strike of shipyard workers in Seattle was violently quelled by federal troops; a similar strike—by policemen—in Boston was crushed, leaving three dead. Strikes by miners and steelworkers received an equally vicious response. The Boston police, mostly conservative and upstanding Irish Catholics, were branded as Bolsheviks. At first, most Americans sympathized with the striking workers. But media propaganda painted the strikers as anti-American reds intent on undermining capitalism, overthrowing the government, and destroying the American way of life. For the most part, the public bought it.

Beginning in April 1919, anarchist militants sent a series of bombs to prominent officials, including mayors and senators, and some individuals were injured. Thirty-four bombs were later intercepted before they went off, but on June 2, a suicide bomber set off a huge explosion that destroyed part of Attorney General Mitchell Palmer's Washington, D.C. home. The perpetrator of the crime was never identified. Undeterred, the government, blaming anarchists and all those on the political left, went into high gear. Palmer, along with the new head of the FBI, J. Edgar Hoover, initiated a series of raids—the Palmer Raids—to ferret out subversives of all kinds, with the goal of having them deported.

In October, agents raided workers' meetings in 12 cities, arresting thousands; 73 "radical" centers in New York City were raided, with 500 arrests. "Red squads" conducted similar raids in cities nationwide. By 1921, 6,000 people had been arrested and 1,000 deported without the constitutionally guaranteed benefit of a trial or hearing.

Robert Benchley, American humorist and newspaper columnist satirized the absurd level of government paranoia and its impact on ordinary citizens in the following essay, which appeared in *The Nation* magazine in 1919.

The Making of a Red
by Robert Benchley

You couldn't have asked for anyone more regular than Peters. He was an eminently safe citizen. . . . There was . . . absolutely nothing in his record which would in the slightest degree alter the true blue of a patriotic litmus. . . .

But one night he made a slip. . . . Shortly before the United States entered the war, Peters made a speech at a meeting of the Civic League. . . . His subject was "Interurban Highways.". . . [I]n the course of his talk, he happened to mention the fact that war, as an institution, has almost always had an injurious effect on public improvements of all kinds. In fact . . . he said that, all things being equal, if he were given his choice of war or peace in the abstract, he would choose peace as a condition under which to live. Then he went on to discuss the comparative values of macadam and wood blocks for paving.

In the audience was a civilian representative of the Military Intelligence Service. He had a premonition that some sort of attempt was being made at this meeting . . . to discredit the war and America's imminent participation therein. And he was not disappointed . . .

Time went by. The United States entered the war, and Peters bought Liberty Bonds. . . . But he did not hear the slow, grinding noise from that district in which are located the mills of the gods. He did not even know there was an investigation going on . . . until he opened his newspaper one morning and . . . [a] glance at the headline chilled [him] . . . "Pro-German List Bared by Army Sleuth."

. . . Peters's eye ran . . . down to the place where . . . was blazoned the name "Horace W. Peters, Pacifist Lecturer.". . . Peters was stunned . . . . [He looked] up some of his friends to explain that there had been a terrible mistake . . . but he was coolly received. No one could afford to be seen talking with him . . . [Someone pointed him out] . . . "That's Peters. Did'je see his name in the papers this morning with them other German spies?". . .

As the days went by, things grew unbelievably worse. He was referred to in public meetings whenever an example of civic treachery was in order . . . [T]he newspaper protest[ed] . . . against the spread of Bolshevism in northern New Jersey, mention[ing] . . . Trotzky [and] Horace W. Peters.

Then something snapped. . . . The last prop of respectability having been removed, the descent was easy. . . . Bolshevik, was he? They had said it! "[W]ho was to blame for this?" he mumbled . . . "Capitalism! Militarism! . . . the damnable bourgeoisie!" . . . He had tried explanations. He had tried argument. There was only one thing left.

You may have read about Peters the other day. He was arrested . . . carrying enough TNT to shift the Palisades back into the Hackensack marshes. . . .

The next morning the Times said, editorially, that it hoped the authorities now saw that the only way to crush Bolshevism was by the unrelenting use of force.

from *The Nation*, March 15, 1919.

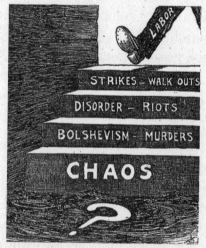

Step by Step, *from* The New York Evening Telegram, *1919. This political cartoon reflects the anxiety and fear that characterized post-war America.*

~ END ~

The Impact of World War I

The end of World War I brought new hope to returning black veterans and to African Americans in general. Many blacks had gotten good jobs in war industries and were beginning to experience some upward mobility, however limited. Returning vets joined the Great Migration north, seeking good jobs and a better life free from the Jim Crow laws of the South. Women, too, enjoyed a sense of power and independence as a result of having entered the workforce to do those jobs that had previously been done by men who had gone overseas to fight. Many women found work in industries supporting the war effort, including factories and shipyards. The war proved that women were as capable as men at doing these jobs, and this realization led eventually to the passage of the 19th Amendment, giving women the vote.

By the 1920s, parts of the nation were high on prosperity. The privations of the war were thrown off, and many (or at least the rich and the upper middle class) dedicated themselves to a hedonistic life of endless fun, good times, and partying.

Flappers became the symbols of the Jazz Age. A flapper was a fairly well-to-do young woman who flaunted her liberation and hedonistic life style in her unmistakable fashion. Flappers cropped their hair short and covered it in sexily slouched cloche hats. They wore short, slinky skirts and turned-down hose, and they powdered their knees and swayed sexily in high heels. Their low-cut tops were often set off by long, loopy necklaces. Flappers were rebels and most definitely "modern." The older generation found the image

Representative T. S. McMillan of Charleston, SC, with flappers, who are doing the Charleston on a railing with the U.S. Capitol Building in the background.

PRIMARY SOURCE: POEM

The Flapper
by Dorothy Parker

The Playful flapper here we see,
  The fairest of the fair

She's not what Grandma used to be—
  You might say *au contraire*.

Her girlish ways may make a stir,
  Her manners cause a scene,

But there is no more harm in her
  Than in a submarine.

She nightly knocks for many a goal
  The usual dancing men.

Her speed is great, but her control
  Is something else again.

All spotlights focus on her pranks,
  All tongues her prowess herald

For which she well may render thanks
  To God and Scott Fitzgerald

Her golden rule is plain enough—
  Just get them young and treat them rough.

〜 END 〜

of the flapper offensive in its blatant sexuality and its often shrill and decidedly less-than-sober determination to have fun. Flappers pursued the high life in dancehalls and nightclubs, where they either wowed or shocked onlookers with the frenetic gyrations of twenties' dance crazes, such as the Charleston. Flapper style was greatly influenced by the movies of the time. Louise Brooks was the ultimate flapper, embodying the flapper lifestyle in her films *Love 'Em & Leave 'Em* (1926), and *Rolled Stockings* (1927).

The twenties also saw the popularization of low-cost fiction, commonly called pulps, because they were printed on cheap paper. For a nickel, you could buy a bodice-ripping romance novel or hard-boiled detective magazine at any newsstand or drugstore. Pulps were the forerunners of today's paperbacks. Many working-class young adults and teenagers were drawn to the medium, which offered escape and entertainment in the form of exotic settings, wild romance, heroic deeds and suspenseful intrigue.

Originating in the 1800s with the work of Edgar Allen Poe, the detective story genre gained a following over the years, particularly with the popularity of British author Sir Arthur Conan Doyle's detective character, Sherlock Holmes. Pulp magazines such as the *Black Mask*, founded by H. L. Mencken and George Jean Nathan in 1920, changed the nature of Doyle's whodunit and the detective himself into a new American creation, crime fiction. Their new hard-boiled detective was a much coarser character, a tough, street-smart man-of-action, with an equal contempt for evildoers and conventional law enforcement.

Science fiction, with its roots in the works of Poe and H. P. Lovecraft, is another genre whose evolution was shaped by the forces of pulp. The magazines *Amazing Stories,* founded in 1926, and *Astounding Science Fiction* made the genre accessible and popular.

Many pulps reinforced strict stereotypes of women. When they weren't selfish sexual predators, they were insipid creatures, focused only on the man of their dreams, who would sweep them off their feet and set them down in the kitchen, where they'd spend the rest of their lives.

Frustration

Despite the image of the carefree flapper, not all was well during the Jazz Age. Frustration and increasing alienation spread among that segment of the population that had not benefited from the postwar boom. Some returning veterans could not find work. The Red Scare, the fear that gripped the nation, the violence, the vicious moralism and bigoted "patriotism"—all were rampant throughout the nation. A deep sense of disillusionment set in, particularly among artists, writers, and intellectuals. World War I had been a bloodbath, whose purpose remained unfathomable to many analysts. Its senseless slaughter made them cynical, and they rejected the "moral values" of the previous generation, which had dragged the world through such a bloody fiasco.

Aided by an advantageous foreign exchange rate, many disillusioned American writers and artists headed for Paris where, they believed, they could create great works free from the suffocating hypocrisy of the United States. These expatriates of the 1920s became known as the "Lost Generation." They formed a bohemian colony of artists on Paris' Left Bank, where they congregated at sidewalk cafes to talk politics, art, and philosophy. Many of them became the literary and artistic lights of their time. They included Ernest Hemingway, John Dos Passos, Ezra Pound, Henry Miller, F. Scott Fitzgerald, Thornton Wilder, and Thomas Wolfe. Most ended up gravitating to the apartment of Gertrude Stein, who ran a kind of informal literary and artistic salon. There they met and hobnobbed with European luminaries like Pablo Picasso. It was Stein who coined the phrase "lost generation," adding that members of this generation had "no respect for anything." By sloughing off traditional morality and dedicating themselves to drinking, debating, and indulging in illicit affairs, the artists of the Lost Generation created an enduring myth, along with a body of literature and art that is among the greatest ever produced.

Copyright © McDougal Littell Inc.

⌒ Notes

_____
_____
_____
_____
_____
_____
_____
_____
_____
_____
_____
_____
_____
_____
_____
_____

The Technology of Progress and Alienation

The prosperity and pursuit of diversion and entertainment in the twenties was fed by new paradigms in industry. During World War I, factories had been set up to mass produce as many munitions or other military supplies as they could possibly churn out. With the end of the war, many industries turned their maximum-output systems toward the manufacture of consumer goods.

By the mid-twenties, wages for many Americans were at an all-time high. The stock market was booming, and Americans were in a spending mood. The decade saw the beginnings of the transformation of the citizen into the consumer. Technology played a significant role in this transformation.

The 1920s was the first decade to be influenced and shaped by mass media. Though still in its infancy, a technological marvel—the radio—was an instant and universal success. Radios were cheap, but if you could not afford to buy one, you could make your own with a battery and a few vacuum tubes for about $2. In 1920, $2 million in radios were sold; by 1929, that number jumped to $600 million. In just a few years, most American homes had a radio.

A technological miracle, the radio brought entertainment, news and advertising straight into the homes of millions of Americans. The first public radio station began broadcasting in 1922 in Pittsburgh, PA.

In 1921, there were 10 radio stations broadcasting nationally; by 1923, there were 350. Tens of millions of people tuned in daily to listen to their favorite shows. Radio had a positive effect insofar as it was a cultural unifier that gave Americans everywhere a common experience. Broadcasts of national events, such as elections and sports, helped create a national identity and linked Americans to one another in a common culture.

Radio also had a negative side. Like all mass media, it could be "addictive." It was also blamed for creating a world of blissful unreality that some Americans preferred to the real world. Further, the world that radio projected was often one that more traditional Americans disdained. Many conservatives blamed radio for an alleged decline of the morals and the patriarchal family they valued.

It did not take long for advertisers to realize the potential of radio for hawking their wares. The first radio ads were broadcast in the twenties, setting the stage for mass media to become the ultimate source for the manufacturing of desire that was essential to the new consumer society. Media and advertising went hand in hand in creating the eternal sense of personal inadequacy and anxiety that was to characterize American mass culture.

Automobiles were a major technological influence on the culture of the twenties. In 1896, Henry Ford started the Ford Motor Company to mass produce inexpensive cars—the Model T— that most people could afford. The automobile transformed both the American psyche and landscape. The car greatly expanded the possibilities for filling up leisure time. Families spent vacations on car trips. Americans began moving to the countryside, soon to become the suburbs. The green landscape was increasingly paved over after the passage of the Federal Road Act in 1924. Mobility became an obsession. It also led to rootlessness. The free-floating anxiety of the times, as well as an expanded range of opportunities for work and leisure, was in no small measure attributable to the automobile.

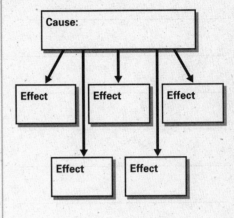

∿ **Notes**

Use a cause and effect diagram to show the different effects cars had on American culture.

Cause:

Effect   Effect   Effect

Effect   Effect

The way in which automobiles were manufactured further contributed to the psychic malaise of the 1920s. Henry Ford perfected the assembly-line system of manufacture but its repetitiveness and monotony reduced the worker to a nameless, faceless cog in the production process. Each worker on the assembly line was responsible for one small action required to manufacture a car. All day every day an assembly line worker might tighten the same screw on each car that passed his station on the line. Henry Ford was hailed as the master of mass production. He paid his workers well and thus enabled them to consume more commodities and lift their standards of living. But his methods, knows as "fordism," dehumanized the workers in his factories and homogenized, or standardized, the goods Americans consumed. Sometimes, technology led to complete mechanization in which the human worker was replaced by a machine that could do the job faster and cheaper and did not require lunch breaks or a weekly salary.

Fordism was a refinement and expansion of the ideas of Frederick Taylor who wrote, in 1911, about how to increase industrial output by "rationalizing" the production process. Taylorism involved time studies of each factory job, analyzing each step in terms of the time spent, the energy expended, and the result. For example, each motion a worker used to tighten a screw was analyzed, and means were found to make this task more efficient. Taylorism led to a severe loss of autonomy among workers, as management clocked each worker's output and penalized or fired those who were too slow. Such practices were detested by workers but they were embraced by corporate managers intent on maximizing efficiency and profits. Taylor was, in effect, the first "efficiency expert."

The dehumanizing effects of the assembly line are eloquently expressed in Charlie Chaplin's 1936 film masterpiece, *Modern Times*.

Boom to Bust: The Great Depression

For a privileged minority, the Roaring Twenties were a boom time of seemingly unlimited optimism. The sky was the limit, and many Americans sought to make their fortune through speculation. Some speculated in land in California and Florida, and many lost their shirts. Undeterred, other Americans poured their wealth into the stock market, though more prudent souls put it in the bank (bank deposits tripled between 1914 and 1928). The Great Bull Market of 1928–1929 was driven by a kind of mass hysteria impelled by greed and the optimistic conviction that anyone and everyone could get rich by buying stock.

By 1929, the stock market dominated the U.S. economy. The problem was that most stocks were bought on margin, a system in which the buyer paid only 10 percent of the stock value, with the remainder of the cost on loan from the stockbroker. By 1929, the broker debt on margin purchases reached $8.5 billion (more than twice the federal budget!). All this debt-financed speculation drove up stock prices but it was empty value, backed by nothing.

Even as he kept advocating the purchase of stock, financier John J. Raskob began selling his stock holdings in early September 1929. The market had been rising dramatically early that month, but by the end of September, it began to slide. Unfazed, some experts claimed that the market had reached a "permanent high plateau." Yet on Thursday, October 24 (Black Thursday), brokers were overwhelmed by orders to sell stock. The market began to fall, but a group of rich investors propped it up by buying. Ordinary stockholders, however, panicked and sought to recoup what they could by selling as many of their shares as possible.

On Black Monday, October 28, the market crashed, with 9.3 million shares being sold at a one-day loss of 13 percent. Black Tuesday (October 29) saw over

_____

_____

_____

_____

_____

_____

_____

_____

_____

_____

_____

_____

_____

_____

The growing economic crisis left millions unemployed. Homeless and jobless, families roamed the country seeking work and shelter, but most communities already had their own financial problems to contend with.

16 million shares traded for a loss of 12 percent. By the end of November investors had lost a total of $100 billion in assets—40 percent of the stock market's value. The stock market would continue to fall until bottoming out in July of 1932 with the Dow at 41.22, down 89.2 percent.

Experts generally agree that the crash of 1929 did not by itself cause the Great Depression that followed. Numerous factors had already weakened the economy to such a point of vulnerability that the crash proved disastrous. Prior to the crash, industrial overproduction put companies in a perilous economic position. After the crash, industrial production fell about 40 perccent. Workers were laid off and unemployment skyrocketed, reaching 12 million by 1931. Panicky depositors rushed to withdraw money from their bank accounts because at that time bank deposits were not federally insured. Many banks, which had invested their depositors' money in the stock market, did not have the cash on hand to return to their customers and were forced to close, bilking their depositors out of their money. In 1930, 1,352 banks failed; by the end of the Great Depression, more than 4,000 would fail, taking many people's life savings with them.

Other factors set the stage for the Depression. Extreme inequality in income (the top 1 percent had incomes 650 perccent greater than the bottom 11 percent) meant that when the market crashed, the discretionary spending of the rich shrank. Had the middle classes had more of the economic pie, their everyday spending might have kept the economy afloat. In 1929, 200 of the largest corporations controlled 50 percent of America's corporate wealth. When the Crash affected one of these companies, it had a far greater impact than it would have if corporate wealth had been evenly distributed.

The Great Depression was a time of extreme privation, even starvation, for millions of Americans. People lost their jobs, their homes, and all their money. Men shamed by their inability to provide abandoned their families and took to the road to look for work that did not exist. Millions subsisted in shantytowns (Hoovervilles named after the

Extreme drought and the over-cultivation of marginal land resulted in dramatic dust storms in the early 1930s that destroyed the livelihood of many mid-western farm families. Many viewed the events as an apocalyptic omen as Woody Guthrie describes in the following song excerpt.

conservative President who did little to jump-start the economy) and on charity. Hoover firmly believed that the burden of aiding the indigent victims of the Depression did not belong to the government, but to the Red Cross, faith-based organizations, and other private charities. Many Americans could see no way out or up; the nation as a whole was hopeless, crushed by despair.

In the early 1930s, bumper crops of wheat and other crops forced farm prices so low that many farmers went broke. To make matters worse, a severe drought struck the Great Plains in the thirties. Farming methods that promoted topsoil erosion, coupled with prolonged lack of rain, caused the soil to blow away in enormous quantities. Between 1934 and 1936, severe dust storms blanketed the plains with clouds of topsoil. Entire towns were buried beneath the blowing dust. The Dust Bowl destroyed the farming economy of the region. Farms had to be abandoned, and many farmers headed west to California (as depicted in John Steinbeck's book, and later the movie, *The Grapes of Wrath*). Many Americans thought it was the end of the world.

PRIMARY SOURCE: SONG

The Great Dust Storm
by Woody Guthrie

On the 14th day of April of 1935,
There struck the worst of dust storms that
    ever filled the sky.
You could see that dust storm comin', the
    cloud looked deathlike black,
And through our mighty nation, it left a
    dreadful track.

From Oklahoma City to the Arizona line,
Dakota and Nebraska to the lazy Rio
    Grande,
It fell across our city like a curtain of black
    rolled down,
We thought it was our judgement, we
    thought it was our doom . . .

It covered up our fences, it covered up our
    barns,
It covered up our tractors in this wild and
    dusty storm.
We loaded our jalopies and piled our
    families in,
We rattled down that highway to never
    come back again.

END

War Abroad and Conflict at Home

EVENTS IN AMERICAN LITERATURE

1940   **1950**   **1960**

1940 John Steinbeck wins Pulitzer Prize in fiction for *The Grapes of Wrath*

1945 Richard Wright details coming of age in *Black Boy*; Randall Jarrell publishes poem "The Death of the Ball Turret Gunner"

1947 Tennessee Williams's *A Streetcar Named Desire* is first produced

1951 J. D. Salinger's novel *Catcher in the Rye* is published

1952 Bernard Malamud publishes baseball novel, *The Natural*

1953 Arthur Miller's *The Crucible*, set during the Salem witch trials in 1692, explores contemporary events surrounding McCarthy hearings

1955 Flannery O'Connor publishes story collection *A Good Man Is Hard to Find*

1961 Joseph Heller's satirical war novel, *Catch-22*, is published

1962 John Steinbeck wins Nobel Prize for literature

1963 Joyce Carol Oates publishes her first book

1969 Kurt Vonnegut publishes *Slaughterhouse-Five*; N. Scott Momaday's *House Made of Dawn* wins Pulitzer Prize

EVENTS IN NORTH AMERICA

1940   **1950**   **1960**

1941 The Japanese bomb Pearl Harbor, bringing United States into World War II

1945 United States drops two atomic bombs on Japan, ending war in Pacific

1950 Senator Margaret Chase Smith addresses Congress, speaking out against McCarthyism

1953 Korean War ends after three years of fighting between Communist troops and UN-sponsored international forces.

1954 Ruling in *Brown* v. *Board of Education*, Supreme Court declares segregated schools unconstitutional

1963 President John F. Kennedy is assassinated in Dallas

1964 Congress passes Civil Rights Act of 1964

1965 First U.S. combat forces land in Vietnam; Malcolm X is assassinated

1967 Thurgood Marshall becomes first African-American justice on Supreme Court

1968 Assassinations of Martin Luther King, Jr., and Robert F. Kennedy

1969 U.S. astronauts land on moon

EVENTS IN THE WORLD

1940   **1950**   **1960**

1940 German forces conquer much of Europe

1945 Germany surrenders to Allies

1948 State of Israel is founded; South African policy of apartheid begins

1949 Communists gain control of China

1957 Soviet Union launches *Sputnik*, first space satellite

1960 Seventeen African countries gain independence

1966 Mao Zedong launches Cultural Revolution in China (to 1976)

1967 Six-Day War erupts between Israel and Arab nations

1970	**1980**	**1990**
1970 Maya Angelou publishes autobiographical *I Know Why the Caged Bird Sings*	**1983** *The House on Mango Street* by Sandra Cisneros is published **1985** Anne Tyler publishes *The Accidental Tourist* **1989** Amy Tan's *The Joy Luck Club* is published	**1990** Tim O'Brien's *The Things They Carried* is published **1993** Toni Morrison wins Nobel Prize for literature

1970	**1980**	**1990**
1974 President Richard M. Nixon resigns to avoid impeachment over Watergate scandal **1975** First successful home VCR appears **1977** First practical home computer, Apple II, hits market	**1981** First space shuttle, *Columbia,* is launched; Sandra Day O'Connor is first woman appointed to U.S. Supreme Court **1989** Oil tanker *Exxon Valdez* runs aground, creating huge oil spill along Alaskan coast	**1991** Persian Gulf War breaks out, and United States leads Allied coalition against Iraq **1995** Murrah Federal Building in Oklahoma City is bombed **1996** Madeleine Albright becomes first woman secretary of state **1997** Unmanned probe *Pathfinder* lands on Mars and sends back pictures **Sept. 11, 2001** Terrorist attack on the United States **March 19, 2003** Second Persian Gulf War begins

1970	**1980**	**1990**
1975 South Vietnam surrenders as North Vietnamese troops occupy Saigon **1979** Egypt's Anwar Sadat and Israel's Menachem Begin sign treaty ending war between Egypt and Israel; Soviet Union invades Afghanistan	**1985** Mikhail Gorbachev comes to power in Soviet Union and initiates reforms **1987** Palestinians begin *intifada* ("shaking off") against Israeli rule **1989** Student demonstrators in China are killed in Tiananmen Square	**1991** Soviet Union breaks up into 15 republics; South Africa begins repeal of apartheid laws **1992** Serbs begin war against Muslims and Croats in former Yugoslavia **1994** Nelson Mandela is elected president of South Africa

∼ Notes

Remembering the Wars

"The internal measures by which a nation attempts to solve its problems are ordinarily of no concern to other nations," Robert Jackson declared in the Opening Address of the Nuremberg Trials in 1946. But the unimaginable atrocities inflicted on Germans by Adolf Hitler, as well as his agenda for total domination of Europe, demanded a global response. Having seized power in 1933, Hitler and the National Socialist German Workers' Party, known as Nazis, sought to avenge Germany's defeat in World War I and to create a new, racially "pure," German state. Surging across Europe, the Nazis targeted specific groups for extermination, most notably Jews, six million of whom were slaughtered in what became known as the Holocaust.

In Asia, Japan's aggressive expansionist government had already seized territories from China and was pushing on to capture the Philippines, Borneo, and several other islands. As part of this campaign for domination, Japanese bombers struck the American naval base at Pearl Harbor, Hawaii, on December 7, 1941, killing over 2,000 Americans. The United States, reacting in fear, banished thousands of Japanese Americans in the United States to internment camps. The U.S. entry into the war turned the tide in favor of the Allies, but it was still a long, hard fight. When the war finally ended in 1945, more than 78 million people had been killed or wounded.

Traditions Across Time

After Pearl Harbor, most Americans supported U.S. participation in World War II, which seemed to threaten the entire free world. Just five years after it ended, the Korean War (1950–1953) began, when Communist North Korea invaded South Korea. With Stalin supporting the North Korean forces and the United States defending the South, the Korean War was the first confrontation between two nuclear powers. Again, the human cost was catastrophic, with an estimated 3.5 million troops dead, missing, or wounded on both sides, and another 2 million civilian deaths in North Korea.

Notes

Fear that Communism would spread, not just abroad but also at home, snowballed throughout the 1940s and 1950s in America. Overshadowed by a growing nuclear arsenal and fueled by a fear of global annihilation, American foreign policy entered a period of entrenchment, with a corresponding hardening towards any sort of political nonconformity at home. This climate of fear and tension proved fertile ground for the zealous anticommunist paranoia of Senator Joseph McCarthy, whose accusations led to one of the most repressive eras in American history.

Twenty years after the Korean War, the United States intervened in South Vietnam to help that republic resist both the Viet Cong and the North Vietnamese army. The longest war in American history, the Vietnam War lasted 18 years and bred a degree of domestic conflict unseen since the Civil War. As the death toll among U.S. soldiers rose—reaching about 58,000 in all—many Americans questioned the wisdom of the United States' presence in Vietnam. Many citizens took to the streets in protest. Meanwhile, African Americans, still struggling for civil rights at home, were being drafted into the military in numbers disproportionate to their numbers in the total population.

The Vietnam War was unique in that it was the first televised war. American opinion on the war was to a large degree shaped by the graphic images of destruction and first-hand accounts of soldiers' experiences shown on the nightly news. The dependence of the public upon these broadcasts made Americans vulnerable to exploitation by those with a vested interest in promoting one side of the story. The highly televised Gulf Wars of 1991 and 2003 are only the latest examples of the interconnectedness of military, corporate, media, and public interests. Several major media networks, owned by conglomerates that benefit from war-related industries, provide citizens with information on world events. With every corporate media merger, the variety of perspectives offered in the media diminishes.

Gunnar Myrdal, distinguished Swedish economist and Nobel Laureate, was commissioned by the Carnegie Corporation in 1938 to study "The American Negro Problem." His findings, published as The American Dilemma, *carried the message that racism was essentially un-American and irrational. His moralistic assessment of America's potential for true equality provided the framework for the Civil Rights movement and shaped current, mainstream perspective on issues of race.*

∽ Notes

_____

_____

_____

_____

_____

_____

_____

_____

_____

War and Racial Equality

At the outbreak of the Second World War, Gunnar Myrdal witnessed the racial scene in the United States and said, "Again the inconsistency between expressed war aims and domestic policy becomes glaring. Again there is discrimination in the Army, Navy, and Air Force, and in the war industries. Again there are Negro heroes, unrecognized by the whites, to be praised." Myrdal's repeated use of the word "again" indicates that the scene he observed in the 1940s was similar to the one that had existed during World War I. The role of African Americans in the military did change dramatically, however, after World War II influenced events in society at large. During and after each war since World War II, the military situation for African American soldiers continued to improve.

World War II (1939–1945)

When the Japanese bombed Pearl Harbor in 1941, African American soldier Dorie Miller shot down four enemy planes and dragged his wounded captain to safety. In spite of such heroism, Miller and other African American soldiers served in an armed service that kept them segregated and limited in number. In response, the African American press, including the *Atlanta Daily World* and the *Chicago Defender,* campaigned for a "double victory"—victory abroad against fascism and victory at home against racism.

As U.S. participation in World War II increased, the government called on industry to provide the needed supplies. War industries, however, would not hire African American workers at first. A. Philip Randolph, head of the sleeping car porters' union, organized a national march on Washington in 1941. Fearful of the disruption, President Roosevelt issued an executive order forbidding job discrimination in war industries. This was a great victory and encouraged many to press for similar gains within the military itself.

Within the military, African Americans eventually formed a successful African American air corps squadron. The 99th Pursuit Squadron, led by Benjamin

Davis Jr. fought next to white soldiers during the decisive Battle of the Bulge. After the war, Randolph organized non-violent resistance against military segregation. Responding to the pressure, President Truman issued an executive order barring segregation in the armed forces.

The Korean War (1950–1953)

Even though Truman had issued his desegregation directive in 1948, the Army, Air Force, Marines, and Navy responded at different rates, with the Army being the most reluctant to integrate. When in 1950 North Korea invaded South Korea, it not only affected Koreans but also the desegregation effort in America.

The United States viewed the North Korean invasion as communist aggression and vowed a swift response. This response provided the opportunity for African Americans to participate for the first time in integrated armed services in large numbers. Although segregation in the military had ended, discrimination had not. When Thurgood Marshall investigated troops for a civil rights organization, he reported that "many of the white officers sneered at their [black] troops. . . . They openly announced: 'I despise nigger troops and I don't want to command you.'"

Soldiers returning home from World War II and the Korean War helped spur on the civil rights movement. African American veterans from World War II had fought fascism bravely and so were treated as equals by Europeans. At home, however, they faced disrespect and substandard living conditions. They expressed their discontent in a variety of ways. Some rioted on army bases in Georgia; others attempted to vote. Meanwhile, Korean War veterans who returned home after having served in an integrated army, cried out for integration at home. The following year, in 1954, the Supreme Court struck down the "separate but equal" philosophy of Jim Crow in its *Brown* v. *Board of Education of Topeka, Kansas* decision.

∿ Notes

As you read, use a cause and effect diagram to write down the events that led to integration of the Armed Forces.

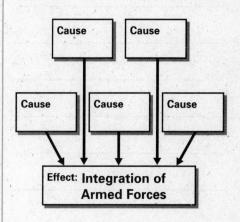

Vietnam War (1957–1975)

While African American soldiers in the Korean War and in preceding wars had sought to increase their numbers in an effort to end discrimination, African American soldiers in the Vietnam War (and in subsequent wars) began to see their increasing numbers as a sign of discrimination. For example, during the Vietnam War, young African American men were drafted at twice the rate of their white counterparts. (White Americans often received educational or other deferments.) African American soldiers, many of whom served on combat tours, also died at higher rates. John Lewis, a civil rights leader, noted that these African American draftees were "called on to stifle the liberation of Vietnam to preserve a 'democracy,' which does not exist for them at home."

After the Vietnam War, and due in part to the criticisms of that war, the U.S. government decorated more African American war heroes than ever before. Typical of those honored was Private Milton Olive, who had thrown himself on a live grenade in order to save others.

In 1971, the military founded the Defense Race Relations Institute that sought to sensitize its officers and personnel to racial issues. In this more open atmosphere, gays also pressed for rights within the military during the 1990s, which resulted in a "don't ask, don't tell" policy. This policy allowed them to serve as long as they remained silent about their sexual orientation.

The Gulf Wars (1991; 2003)

As racial tensions eased in the new volunteer military, African Americans and other minorities signed up, often finding more opportunity for advancement in the armed services than in non-unionized industries.

Still, many questioned the high ratio of African Americans in the military. During the second Gulf War, Representative Charles Rangel sponsored a reinstatement of the draft, stating that all races should share equally in national defense. General Colin Powell and others, however, argued that the best way to reduce the high ratio of African American soldiers was for "the rest of American society [to] open its doors to African Americans. . . ."

The Cold War and McCarthyism

Having had Germany as a common enemy during the war, the Soviet Union found itself among the Allies after World War II. However, the Soviet Union's ideological differences and its aspiration for nuclear weapons were soon seen by the U.S. as a serious threat to world peace. The Soviet Union, which controlled most of eastern Europe, also had strong ties to Communist China and Korea. Corporate America, which had struggled through bleak financial times in the 1930s, had learned a critical lesson from World War II that contributed to the growing anti-Soviet sentiment in the U.S.; the lesson was that a war economy meant profits and economic stability. An arms race had economic merit.

The resulting decades-long standoff between the Soviet Union and America became known as the Cold War. Domestically, the early part of that era became known as the McCarthy Era, named after Senator Joseph R. McCarthy, a fanatical anti-communist whose aggressive and often unfounded accusations against citizens and government officials ruined many lives and careers. Immigrants in America, along with American Communist Party members and other left-leaning citizens, lived in an atmosphere of suspicion and hostility. McCarthy was relentless in his efforts to identify and eradicate potential sources of communist propaganda.

The Alien Registration Act of 1940, which made it a crime to advocate overthrowing the U.S. government, was often invoked during the Cold War. In 1950, the Internal Security Act was passed, which required the registration of organizations believed to be communist-affiliated, along with a detention camp bill authorizing the creation of detention centers for suspected subversives.

McCarthyism had a chilling effect on free expression, especially in the film industry. Many Hollywood stars and directors were called before the House Un-American

Notes

As you read this selection, use a cause and effect chart to examine the effects of McCarthyism.

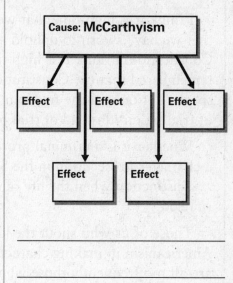

Declaration of Conscience

Margaret Chase Smith, June 1, 1950

I think it is high time that we remembered that we have sworn to uphold and defend the Constitution. I think it is high time that we remembered that the Constitution, as amended, speaks not only of the freedom of speech but also of trial by jury instead of trial by accusation.

Whether it is a criminal prosecution in court or a character prosecution in the Senate, there is little . . . distinction when the life of a person has been ruined.

Those of us who shout the loudest about Americanism in making character assassinations are all too frequently those who . . . ignore some of the basic principles of Americanism:

- The right to criticize;
- The right to hold unpopular beliefs;
- The right to protest;
- The right of independent thought.

The exercise of these rights should not cost one single American citizen his reputation or his right to a livelihood nor should he be in danger of losing his reputation or livelihood because he happens to know someone who holds unpopular beliefs. Who of us doesn't? Otherwise none of us could call our souls our own. Otherwise thought control would have set in.

from *Congressional Record of the Senate, 81st Congress, 2nd Session, June 1, 1950*

∾ END ∾

Activities Committee (HUAC), a committee that investigated charges of treason. In 1952 Elia Kazan, a well-known Hollywood movie director, was called before HUAC. He decided to name eight theater workers who had been members of the Communist Party with him in the 1930s. Refusing to betray others would have resulted in being blacklisted, which meant being prevented from working in the film industry. Kazan justified his decision by saying that he truly believed that Communism had become a threat to the U.S.

Kazan's friend Arthur Miller began writing *The Crucible* at about the time that Kazan testified. *The Crucible*, a play that dramatizes the hysteria of the 17th-century Salem witch hunts, can be read as an allegory of McCarthy's persecution of suspected communists. Later, Miller appeared before HUAC but refused to implicate anyone other than himself. This oppressive atmosphere moved Republican Senator Margaret Chase Smith of Maine to address Congress on June 1, 1950 with her Declaration of Conscience.

∾ Notes

_____

_____

_____

_____

The Impact of the Electronic Media on News Events

McCarthyism and Televised Hearings

Television, which became available in many homes during the 1950s, precipitated the downfall of Joseph McCarthy. As viewers watched the Congressional hearings, McCarthy's bombastic attacks on the accused alienated and enraged the public. Even the *New York Times* disparaged "the television carnival produced, staged, and directed by Senator McCarthy."

War Coverage: Vietnam

The words "produced, staged, and directed" draw attention to the way television as a medium can be manipulated. By playing up certain events, television experts can "stage" a drama or "produce" a visually and verbally powerful story. Many critics deemed television's presentation of the Vietnam war to be a benchmark by which subsequent coverage of world events should measure and adjust itself.

According to media critic Daniel C. Hallin, the way the media covered Vietnam changed during the course of the war. Before 1968, correspondents reported events using the word "our" as in *our forces, our efforts,* thus closely aligning the media with government objectives. Correspondents compared the Vietnam War to World War II, a war that most citizens considered justified and triumphant. In World War II, reporters never personalized body counts by having survivors remember their fallen comrades. After 1968, however, when the war no longer had popular support, the press ceased using the possessive adjective *our* in their reports. They no longer talked about "winning the war." They began to personalize body counts with film of startling war images. Many military officers felt that these images, and the civilian indignation they evoked, contributed to military failure.

In a Venn diagram, show the ways in which media coverage of various events had points in common and ways in which they remained distinct.

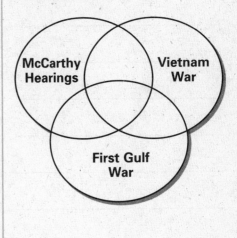

War Coverage: The First Gulf War

Remembering what had happened in Vietnam, war "planners" set out to control the media's "story" during the first Gulf War in 1991, which was the first war televised in "real time." There was a conscious effort to manufacture consensus rather than cultivate it. Such efforts included media images of a "Hitler-like" Saddam Hussein and unsubstantiated allegations of atrocities committed by Iraqi troops. The military implemented a system whereby journalists would travel with the troops, embedded into specific units. One skeptical reporter remarked that this procedure essentially turned the journalist into "an unpaid employee of the Department of Defense." Many reporters bonded with "their" units, and again used words such as *our troops, our efforts,* instead of trying to maintain objectivity. Because few photographers were free to travel on their own, they did not film casualties. Instead the media showed smart bombs hitting their targets, in footage prepared by the military.

Conglomerates

Conglomerates may also have contributed to this supportive treatment of that war by the media. During the 1980s, media companies merged into conglomerates, such as Time Warner and News Corporation. These large companies held interests in such diverse areas as entertainment, sports, real estate, and electrical appliances. These conglomerates applied advertising techniques to journalism, so that spectacle, repetition, and pacing became more important than in-depth analysis. More than ever before, journalism was now part of an economic mix and had to prove its moneymaking ability by putting on dazzling shows for viewers. In this new atmosphere, critics of these changes feared stories would become more simplistic, less nuanced. Greg Dyke, of the British Broadcasting Corporation, criticized U.S. media for "swap[ping] impartiality for patriotism" after the terrorist attacks of September 11, 2001 in New York City and Washington, D.C., and during the second Gulf War of 2003. The Internet and independent films, however, offered alternative, more critical, in-depth news coverage.

Integration and Disintegration

American literature after World War II reflects the many changes that took place in society during that time. On one hand, African Americans, Latinos, women, and other groups previously excluded from political and cultural participation were increasingly integrated into mainstream society. On the other hand, the structures and values that had once been upheld in the nation were disintegrating, replaced with more relevant, modern ideas.

The enduring image of American society in the 1950s is that of a prosperous, consumerist, and conformist culture. Popular culture both celebrated that state of affairs and rebelled against it. Television shows of the 1950s idealized family life, with authoritarian fathers, soothing mothers, and mischievous but obedient children. The female characters were housewives and mothers, and spent their days cooking and housecleaning. The children were loved and pampered. The husband-father was a responsible businessman and perfect citizen, dispensing sage advice to his brood at the dinner table. David Halberstam observed, "It was the television images of the era that remained so remarkably sharp in people's memories, often fresher than memories of real life."

While these TV families embodied the prosperity, consumerism, and conformity of the 1950s, they ignored the repressive dark side of the era. In real life, some pampered upper middle-class children emerged as restless adolescents. Popular music provided an outlet and an identity for teenagers. Previous generations had not thought of adolescence as a "life stage," but only as the time in life to accept adult responsibility. For the first time in the prosperous 1950s, youth had the disposable income necessary to distinguish itself from adulthood and even stand in opposition to it. While middle-class adults often listened to cheerful hit parade ditties such as "If I Knew You Were Coming, I'd Have Baked a Cake,"

_____

_____

_____

_____

_____

_____

_____

_____

_____

_____

_____

_____

_____

_____

_____

_____

_____

_____

some of their teenage sons and daughters began to tune in radio stations playing the rhythm and blues of African American artists. Perceiving a trend, white disc jockeys and music producers soon found ways to tailor this "forbidden" music to the ears of the majority of white teenagers who had money to buy records. Promoters dubbed the new music "rock and roll," a term from the ghetto meaning "dancing and sex." Many white singers recorded African American songs, often copying them in almost all details except for censoring sexual innuendos possibly too explicit for white audiences. However, in time, innovative white singers emerged. The most phenomenal star of this group was Elvis Presley, whose gyrations and flamboyance outraged parents but gave voice to the yearnings of millions of teenagers. At the same time, the term "juvenile delinquent" gained currency and cinematic personification in such films as *The Wild One, Rebel without a Cause*, and *Blackboard Jungle*, the last of which made a point of linking rock and roll music to "juvenile delinquent" behavior.

In the 1960s, an influential youth counterculture arose, best characterized perhaps by the tenet, "Do Your Own Thing." Popular music, some imported from the United Kingdom, highlighted such groups as the Beatles and the Rolling Stones, both of which drew inspiration from African American rhythm and blues music. As some parts of society became more permissive, the family as an institution weakened and parents were losing authority over children.

Literature, like society in general, reacted to the post-war forces of conformity and civil rights issues. The 1950s' literary establishment was slow to embrace socially aware literature. The Beats, however, pushed literary boundaries with their innovative writing and lifestyles and were, in that sense, avant-garde. Jack Kerouac, one of the most well-known Beat writers defined the Beats as ". . . a generation of furtives. You know, with an inner knowledge . . . a kind of beatness . . . and a weariness with all the forms, all the conventions of the world. . . . So I guess you might say we're a 'Beat Generation.'"

At that time, a variety of ethnic voices was also beginning to gain recognition in the literary establishment. As early as the 1950s, Jewish writer Saul Bellow described the ordinary life of Jewish immigrants, while Flannery O'Connor expressed a regional southern point of view. In addition, within a decade, Mexican American farm workers and students, Native Americans, Asian Americans, feminists, the disabled, and many other Americans demanded basic rights and complete equality to express their particular cultural identities in poems, drama, and fiction. Defining one's identity became a common theme, from Gary Soto's poem "Mexicans Begin Jogging" to Alice Walker's *The Color Purple*.

African American writers continued to depict the realities of urban life and political anger throughout the turbulent fight for civil rights, which reached its peak between 1955 and 1965. Like other ethnic groups establishing their literary identity, African American writers found increasing acceptance and recognition of their talent within the mainstream.

The inclusion of disparate voices within the literary establishment characterizes the postmodern literary world in which the fragmentation and despair of modernism is reconstructed in an eclectic pastiche of elements and styles. Strange juxtapositions, fragmentation, contradictory voices, and a desire to expose historical stereotypes also reflect the postmodern trend. These same characteristics are seen in all realms of postmodern expression, including architecture, which seeks to incorporate disorienting and kinetic spaces within a design. Postmodern advertising focuses on playful, "feel good" virtual experiences of the consumer rather than on any qualities of the actual products. While many celebrate the virtual as real, others face the complex realities of modern life requiring social action and citizen participation.

∼ Notes

As you read this section, take notes on the similarities and differences between the nonviolent approach and the militant approach to civil rights activism.

Approaches to Activism	
Compare	Contrast

The Civil Rights Movement

Based on [my] knowledge of Georgians North and South, Rural and Urban, liberal and conservative, I say to you quite frankly that the time for racial discrimination is over. Our people have already made this major and difficult decision, but we cannot underestimate the challenge of hundreds of minor decisions yet to be made.

Jimmy Carter's words as he took the office of governor in 1971 were a testimony to his vision for true equality in Georgia. The U.S., and the South in particular, had made great progress, but much remained to be done. His words had been preceded by decades of protests, marches, sit-ins, boycotts, and debates—protest actions united by the common cause of civil rights, yet based on two distinct underlying approaches to the attainment of the goal. These approaches can be classified as:

- nonviolent resistance, influenced by the African American Christian church;
- militant resistance, influenced by the Nation of Islam, Marxist ideology, and ghetto uprisings.

Nonviolent Resistance

Martin Luther King Jr.'s approach to activism was informed by the philosophy of nonviolence. As a young man, King had been inspired by Henry David Thoreau's essay "Civil Disobedience." Later, he attended a lecture on Mahatma Gandhi and began reading about his life and works. As a child, King had been steeped in the teachings of Jesus Christ. Reading about Gandhi, he began to recognize that Jesus's admonition to "love thy neighbor," had applications in the real world as well on the personal level. His philosophy of political nonviolence influenced his leadership of boycotts and marches in the fight for civil rights. As his famous "I Have A Dream" speech illustrates, King's vision although non-violent, was one of impassioned, continuous action.

PRIMARY SOURCE: SPEECH

I Have A Dream

Martin Luther King, August 28, 1963

Nineteen sixty-three is not an end but a beginning. Those who hope that the Negro needed to blow off steam and will now be content will have a rude awakening if the nation returns to business as usual.

There will be neither rest nor tranquility in America until the Negro is granted his citizenship rights. The whirlwinds of revolt will continue to shake the foundations of our nation until . . . justice emerges. . . .

Let us not seek to satisfy our thirst for freedom by drinking from the cup of bitterness and hatred. We must ever conduct our struggle on the high plane of dignity and discipline. We must not allow our creative protest to degenerate into physical violence. . . . And as we walk, we must make the pledge that we shall always march ahead. We cannot turn back.

END

Two of the most influential civil rights leaders, Martin Luther King Jr. and Malcolm X, held opposing views on how to achieve racial equality in American society. King advocated non-violent resistance and civil disobedience, while Malcolm X urged African Americans to fight oppression "by any means necessary."

Notes

Militant Resistance: Malcolm X

Concurrent with the work of Martin Luther King, other black activists were frustrated over the failure of the Civil Rights Movement to focus on the needs of urban African Americans. Many also objected to having whites as leaders in the various black organizations. From these frustrations, the Black Power movement arose, advocating separatist action as a means of reclaiming power in an oppressively racist society.

Black Power not only advocated separatism, but also the use of militant armed resistance as a response to discrimination against African Americans. The militant views of activist Robert F. Williams shaped the philosophy of the Black Power movement. His work, *Negroes With Guns,* profoundly impacted Huey P. Newton, Malcolm X, and others. Under the leadership of Malcolm X, the Nation of Islam sought to attain a separate black state, using whatever means necessary.

_____

_____

_____

_____

_____

_____

_____

_____

_____

_____

_____

_____

_____

_____

_____

_____

_____

PRIMARY SOURCE: AUTOBIOGRAPHY

From *The Autobiography of Malcolm X*

I *am* for violence if non-violence means we continue postponing a solution to the American black man's problem—just to *avoid* violence. I don't go for non-violence if it also means a delayed solution. To me a delayed solution is a non-solution. Or I'll say it another way. If it must take violence to get the black man his human rights in this country, I am *for* violence exactly as you know the Irish, the Poles, or Jews would be if they were flagrantly discriminated against. I am just as they would be in that case, and they would be for violence—no matter what the consequences, no matter who was hurt by the violence. . . .

Well, it may be that the American black man does need to become involved in a *real* revolution. The word for revolution in German is *Umwälzung*. What it means is a complete overturn—a complete change.

~ *END* ~

In the late 1960s, following a series of race riots in cities across the country, the Black Panther Party took up the call for militant "black power." Originating in Oakland, CA, the group soon garnered a nationwide following as racial tensions escalated. Their affiliation with Marxist ideology further contributed to their extremist image. The FBI cracked down on the group, killing many of its leaders, and destroying its ability to function. Black Power, however, continued as a motivating force in many black communities.

A decade after the demise of the militant movement, the quest for equal rights and racial harmony continues amidst ever-increasing ethnic diversity.

New Voices in America

After World War II, just as the civil rights movement began to emerge, new voices within American literature also began to emerge. Within the atmosphere of conformity and Cold War, much of the literary establishment in the 1950s was conservative and insular. It was the era of "New Criticism," an approach to literature that ignored the world at large in favor of the text itself. In addition, the favored texts were by an elite group, entrenched in universities, whose writing appeared in prestigious journals such as *The Kenyon Review, The Hudson Review,* and *The Partisan Review.* Critics of this era ignored or disparaged writers who did not share their aesthetic concerns—writers including women, immigrants, Jews, African Americans, and bohemians (artists who lived on the fringe of society). Nonetheless, in time, these ignored authors gained readership and currency. In the 1950s, for example, some bohemians, called Beats—Allen Ginsberg, Jack Kerouac, Lawrence Ferlinghetti, and others—organized poetry readings, opened bookstores, and established publishing venues of their own. Influenced by the rhythms and experimentation of jazz, the Beats included African Americans, such as Leroi Jones (later called Amiri Baraka) in their ranks. Like the new "rock and roll" stars, they could also connect with white alienated youth. Allen Ginsberg, a key figure in the Beat movement, gave voice to such marginal groups as homosexuals, drug addicts, the mentally ill, Leftists, and disaffected Jews, in such works as *Howl* (1956). In fact, he was one of many new Jewish writers, including Saul Bellow and Philip Roth, who found their voices beginning in the 1950s.

Meanwhile in the South, the Southern Renaissance, which had first blossomed in the 1920s, found new energy. But this time it was white women—Flannery O'Connor, Carson McCullers, Eudora Welty—not men, who often took the lead. Soon African American women's voices, such as Maya Angelou (*I Know Why the Caged Bird Sings,* 1970) and Toni Morrison (*The Bluest Eye,* 1970), also moved to the forefront. By

~ Notes

Use a cluster chart to identify and take notes about some of the new voices in American literature.

New Voices in American Literature

Copyright © McDougal Littell Inc.

_____

_____

_____

_____

_____

_____

_____

_____

_____

_____

_____

_____

_____

_____

_____

_____

_____

_____

the 1980s, identity literature was the rule rather than the exception. Throughout the country, immigrant authors, such as Li-Young Lee (*The City in Which I Love You*, 1990) and Jamaica Kinkaid (*At the Bottom of the River*, 1985) eagerly shared their unique perspectives. At the same time, Native American novelists and poets, such as Leslie Marmon Silko (*Ceremony*, 1984) sought to renew their links with the past and to find their role in postmodern society.

New Southern Voice: Flannery O'Connor

Flannery O'Connor was born in Savannah, Georgia in 1925. Born Catholic, in the Protestant "Bible belt," O'Connor viewed the world around her with an outsider's perspective. Her gender and southern regionalism also contributed to her role as an outsider in the American literary establishment.

As a young woman, O'Connor had read William Faulkner and other southern authors of the previous generation. Unlike Faulkner, O'Connor did not dwell on the Civil War and the guilt associated with slavery. She saw racism as part of the complacency of the people she observed around her, which she equated with evil. In "A Good Man Is Hard to Find," for example, the character of the grandmother lives her quotidian life by reciting clichés, including racist ones. This character is only redeemed when a misfit inflicts shocking violence upon her and her family, thereby forcing her to see beyond banality. The story is an absurd mixture of humor and violence, a "grotesque" blend that defines O'Connor's Southern Gothic style. In a tribute to O'Connor, Alice Walker noted that the "*essential* O'Connor is not about race at all . . . If it can be said to be 'about' anything, then it is . . . 'about' the impact of supernatural grace on human beings who don't have a chance of spiritual growth without it."

African American Voice: Alice Walker

Alice Walker, like Flannery O'Connor, was born in Georgia, but two decades later (in 1944), and under more impoverished circumstances. Her parents sharecropped in rural Georgia, and Alice was the youngest of eight children. Although a bright child, Walker became shy and withdrawn after one of her brothers accidentally shot her in the eye. The incident set her apart from her peers and influenced her perspective as an outsider within her own society. In the 1960s, Alice Walker began publishing her work. She gained greatest recognition more than a decade later at a time when African American women's literature flowered.

Walker's most famous novel, *The Color Purple,* explores various controversial themes—incest, rape, segregation, homosexuality, sexual awakening, and identity—through letters that the main character, Celie, an abused, stunned ingénue, writes to God. In *The Color Purple,* Walker manages to integrate concerns of the women's movement with concerns of the civil rights movement in a style that draws upon dialect and ancestral folk wisdom.

Native American Voice: N. Scott Momaday

N. Scott Momaday also draws upon ancestral folk wisdom in his famous *The Way to Rainy Mountain.* Born in 1934 in Oklahoma of Kiowa Indian heritage, Momaday sought to meld native folktales with modern fiction. Western author and naturalist Edward Abbey described Momaday's "quest for roots" as a journey that took him to "the hills of Kentucky and north to the high plains of Wyoming, and . . . back to the Bering Straits." The very geography of Momaday's work signaled that he was a new voice in American literature, which before the 1950s promoted mainly Eastern and Midwestern authors.

In one section of *The Way to Rainy Mountain,* Momaday relates a folktale about a talking dog that served the Kiowa people at a time when they did not have horses. Later he links this folktale with a historical narrative, and then to a childhood memory of the "nameless" dogs in his grandmother's house. "They belonged there in a sense that the word 'ownership' does not include," he wrote. Momaday's juxtaposition of folktale, historical record, and personal observation marks his work as postmodern.

Postmodernism

Compared to previous historical periods, America in the new millennium is a complex society filled with skepticism, fragmentation, diversity, and subjectivity. Postmodernism is a term that encompasses all aspects of culture, including art, architecture, music, film, literature, fashion, technology, communication and more. While it shares many traits with modernism, such as an emphasis on subjectivity, a preference for discontinuous narratives, a rejection of formal aesthetics, and an affinity for irony, the attitude underlying postmodernism is in essence quite different. Whatever its form of expression, the postmodern celebrates the deconstructive aspects of reality. Postmodern writers and artists have no desire to construct order from chaos, or to unify reality into a "grand narrative."

One characteristic of postmodern literature is to view history critically, not as an objective force from the past but as a source of individual narratives shaped by the needs of the present. For example, in *Beloved*, Toni Morrison revisits the horrors of slavery, retelling its story from the multiple points of view of recently emancipated slaves. In *Dreaming in Cuban*, Cristina Garcia uses contradictory points of view to reconstruct the Cuban Revolution and its aftermath. These novels are not simply historical; through the narrative, the authors explore contemporary feminist concerns. Such a melding of past and present is typical of postmodernism.

Unusual juxtaposition (placing disparate items next to each other without any explanation), another postmodern characteristic, can be seen in the work of Thomas Pynchon, Richard Bratigan, and Don DeLillo. For example, in DeLillo's novel *White Noise* (1985), the author abruptly interjects news headlines or soap opera dialogue into his narrative to draw attention to the role media plays in our lives. Postmodernism is a complex term that describes one approach to the world we live in today. An examination of the way the term is used in architecture and in advertising will further illustrate its various meanings.

Architecture

As with literature, postmodern architecture concerns itself with history, but often in an exuberant melding of periods and styles. Modern architecture clearly looked toward the future and eschewed the past, refusing to adhere to any historical style or conceal the structure with historical decoration. Modernists preferred the honesty and integrity of the unadorned structure: its bare structure is its design and beauty.

Postmodernists, however, find such bare-bone buildings monotonous. Mocking modernist Mies van der Rohe's dictum "less is more," postmodernist Robert Venturi quipped, "less is a bore." The historical reference in postmodern buildings is a pastiche that mixes and matches styles and periods, creating an architectural expression of irony. For example, Venturi's Franklin Court in Philadelphia references both pop art and traditional American residential architecture, but using a typically modern material: stainless steel. The work has mass appeal and humorously pays homage to its surroundings by alluding to Benjamin Franklin's home.

Advertising

Dislocation also distinguishes postmodern advertising: the advertised product often absents itself from the scene. Freed from the products, playful and enigmatic ads entertain and seduce the viewer while seeming only to celebrate their own creativity. The ads reflect the postindustrial society's dependence on intangibles, such as services, entertainment, and technology (rather than actual products.) Some corporations that do produce tangible products sell their products online, in a virtual store, where the physical meets the nonphysical, and the company is able to retain its traditional brand recognition.

While some critics see in postmodern consumerism the potential for the unlimited acquisition of goods to fill a void left by the fragmentation of society and its values, others see in postmodernism an escape from the culture of consumption. In rejecting the "grand narratives" of historical social struggles and focusing instead on the particular and the local, an individual is able to effectively undertake social change.

The Renaissance Center in Detroit, MI, exemplifies John Portman's postmodern architecture. Portman's hotels make no attempt to fit into the surroundings, but rather provide an alternative universe. Their reflective glass and unannounced entrances do not invite a dialogue with the surrounding cityscape. With spiral staircases, serpentine passageways and disorienting expansive spaces, Portman's hotels offer visitors an unsettling dislocation from the human body and physical space, not unlike the cyberspace of the Internet.

∼ Notes

_____

_____

_____

_____

_____

Multiple Choice Questions

Write the letter of the best answer. This exercise is continued on the next page.

_____ 1. What is the main way in which Native American literature is distinct from the literature of European Americans?

a. Native American literature retains a much closer association with oral and ceremonial rituals than does European American literature.

b. Native American literature always included ceremonial songs and stories.

c. Unlike Native American literature, Western literature's origins are unknown.

d. All Western literature began exclusively as nonfiction.

_____ 2. What does the name the Cherokee chose for themselves—"the Principal People"—say about their view of their own culture?

a. They wanted to live under the rule of the Iroquois.

b. They saw all people as equal, including other populations of Native Americans.

c. They considered themselves to be the first and central group of people on Earth.

d. They believed that they were the only people who lived on Earth.

_____ 3. What was the most important function of songs in Native American culture?

a. They provided a means of entertainment and a focus at celebrations.

b. Songs were central to religious ceremonies and passed along cultural traditions.

c. Songs were sung before hunts and wars and used to relate events after the fact.

d. They provided a means for Native Americans to express their love for one another and the earth.

_____ 4. What main thread runs through the literature that describes the European exploration of the Americas?

a. Most of it is written in letter form to family members and friends at home.

b. All of it focuses on the explorers, not the natives, and it does not provide any idea of the people encountered.

c. All of it contains great exaggerations about the dangers of the high seas and the encounters with natives.

d. Most of it represents European values as natural and native values as perverse or exotic.

5. What is the purpose of the story of the Great Buzzard in "How the World Was Made"?

   a. It tells why the Cherokee worshipped the Great Buzzard.

   b. It explains why the Cherokee land was mountainous.

   c. It serves as a reminder to be kind to animals.

   d. It expresses the belief that buzzards are useful animals.

6. What is an implied warning, not a stated moral, of "Coyote and the Another One"?

   a. Don't let other people define who you are.

   b. Move toward solidarity in your opposition to outsiders.

   c. Beware of people who claim to be like you or related to you.

   d. Address all your relatives with respect.

7. Which of the following is an example of Coyote's paradoxical nature?

   a. He has no values yet teaches values.

   b. He often appears in creation myths.

   c. He can change into different shapes.

   d. He tricks people and animals.

8. How does Columbus's first encounter with natives, which was marked with "mistaken identity and injury," foreshadow events to come in the history of exploration?

   a. It establishes the Europeans as more intelligent than the indigenous people.

   b. It suggests that the indigenous people were planning to revolt from the beginning.

   c. It warns of the damage that will be inflicted upon the native peoples.

   d. It addresses the introduction of firearms into the native communities.

9. What specific event precipitated the European Age of Discovery?

   a. Europeans had long wanted to colonize foreign lands and trade slaves.

   b. Most Europeans heard rumors of a new world across the Atlantic.

   c. Christians hoped to proselytize to worldwide regions.

   d. The land route to the East had been cut off by wars with the Turks.

_____ **10.** Which best describes the style of writing of William Bradford's *History of Plymouth Plantation*?

    a. He uses strictly scientific descriptions.

    b. He tells a sparse narrative with only the bare facts.

    c. He presents a romanticized tale of the settlers' lives.

    d. He gives a realistic account of life in the colonies.

Short Answer Questions

Answer the following questions on the lines provided.

1. In what ways did the white settlers' attitudes toward Native Americans change with time, and how did this change in outlook exemplify the basic values that they carried with them to their new country?

2. What were some of the ways that explorers represented the people and cultures native to the Americas, and how did their contradictory attitudes provide evidence of their ethnocentrism?

3. What purpose did spirituals and trickster tales serve in the culture created and maintained by enslaved African Americans?

4. What were the various roles played by oral traditions in Native American culture, and how did the practice of these traditions buttress the basic worldviews of these cultures?

5. How are we, as contemporary English readers, removed from traditional Native American texts, and what can we do to bridge the gap in understanding that this creates?

_____
_____
_____

Summary Questions

Answer the following questions on the lines provided.

1. What are the main kinds of Native American literature, and what functions do they serve?

_____
_____
_____
_____
_____
_____
_____

2. Summarize the explanation given for the earth's terrain in the creation myth "How the World Was Made."

_____
_____
_____
_____
_____
_____
_____

3. What are the main purposes of songs in the Native American culture, and how does "The Song of the Lenape Warriors Going Against the Enemy" exemplify these purposes?

    _____

    _____

    _____

    _____

    _____

    _____

4. Explain why Africans were brought to the New World and how they were treated once they arrived.

    _____

    _____

    _____

    _____

    _____

    _____

5. Summarize William Bradford's account of the first Thanksgiving.

    _____

    _____

    _____

    _____

    _____

    _____

    _____

Multiple Choice Questions

Write the letter of the best answer. This exercise is continued on the next page.

_____ 1. What was a main factor that strained the relationship between Native Americans and Puritans?

    a. The two groups vied for the allegiance of the Canadians.

    b. The two groups wanted to explore the same territories in the West.

    c. The two groups differed in their concepts of land ownership.

    d. The two groups disagreed about how Catholicism should be practiced.

_____ 2. How was John Williams's captivity experience different from that of Mary Rowlandson?

    a. He experienced excellent treatment at the hands of Native Americans.

    b. He was not separated from the rest of his family members.

    c. He ended up dying while in captivity with the French Canadians.

    d. He resisted religious conversion while he was held captive.

_____ 3. What was a possible motivation for the teenaged girls in Salem becoming bewitched?

    a. The girls were actually afflicted with smallpox and suffered delusions.

    b. The girls had moved away from their families and needed a diversion.

    c. The girls were engaging in forbidden activities and felt guilty.

    d. The girls were trying to avoid going to public school and religious services.

_____ 4. What was John Edward's contribution to The Great Awakening?

    a. He considered religion and science incompatible.

    b. He combined religion with current intellectual movements.

    c. He used the arguments of John Locke to strengthen his writings.

    d. He attacked preachers for fear they were destroying the church.

_____ 5. What was the final result of The Great Awakening?

    a. New religious groups and increased religious tolerance developed.

    b. People started to believe they were doomed to damnation.

    c. Preachers became wealthy and desired as national speakers.

    d. Colonists hysterically accused one another of witchcraft.

_____ 6. In what way did Abigail Adams contribute to her husband's efforts?

   a. She was embarrassed by her lack of formal education and poor spelling.

   b. She toured the country on his behalf, speaking out on major issues.

   c. She encouraged him to visit Native Americans and create alliances with them.

   d. She took care of their farm and children while he served the nation.

_____ 7. Which key issue was not addressed by colonists during the American Revolution?

   a. The colonists failed to discuss how the new government would be set up.

   b. The colonists ignored the pressing question of slavery in the new nation.

   c. The colonists did not fully understand the concept of natural rights.

   d. The colonists were ill-equipped to fight against the British.

_____ 8. Why did the efforts of James Oglethorpe fail in Georgia?

   a. He initiated restrictions that thwarted growth and that the new settlers eventually resisted.

   b. He was unable to get financing for the new colony.

   c. He was not adept at attracting ministers to settle in the South.

   d. He did not get along well with the region's Native Americans.

_____ 9. Which of the following statements best defines indentured servitude?

   a. Indentured servitude involves the exchange of land for labor.

   b. Indentured servitude involves working to pay off travel costs.

   c. Indentured servitude involves slavery of people from Africa.

   d. Indentured servitude involves unjust imprisonment of debtors.

_____ 10. Which answer best describes the feelings of colonial women during the time of the American Revolution?

   a. They were relieved that they did not have to fight against the British.

   b. They were frightened and wanted to return to the safety of England.

   c. They were astonished by the hard conditions and the lack of food and supplies.

   d. They were eager to contribute to the Revolution on and off the battlefield.

Short Answer Questions

Answer the following questions on the lines provided.

1. Describe how Puritan women were viewed in society.

   _____

   _____

   _____

   _____

2. How did the Puritans show their intrinsic goodness after the Salem Witch Trials?

   _____

   _____

   _____

   _____

3. What were the significant qualities of John Edwards's writing and sermonizing?

   _____

   _____

   _____

   _____

4. How did Locke's writing and the Bible contribute to the growing need for revolution among the colonists?

   _____

   _____

   _____

   _____

5. In what way did Crèvecoeur differ from Franklin in his perspective on the colonists?

_____

_____

_____

_____

Summary Questions

Answer the following questions on the lines provided.

1. How could the stereotypical view of Puritans best be refuted?

_____

_____

_____

_____

_____

_____

2. Which activities and writings exemplified the intellectual richness of Puritan society?

_____

_____

_____

_____

_____

_____

3. In what way do the captivity narratives reinforce the Puritan view of the world?

    _____

    _____

    _____

    _____

    _____

4. Why was Jonathan Edwards seen as a symbol of the transition between historical periods?

    _____

    _____

    _____

    _____

    _____

    _____

5. Discuss some of the people most responsible for the growing belief that revolution was inevitable, and describe their contributions.

    _____

    _____

    _____

    _____

    _____

    _____

Multiple Choice Questions

Write the letter of the best answer. This exercise is continued on the next page.

_____   1. What characteristics are typically found in the writings of the Romantics?

     a. The setting is always dark and frightening.

     b. There is a focus on nature and the self.

     c. They most often center around an exploration of mental illness.

     d. The focus is on descriptions of landscapes.

_____   2. Which of the following tasks was NOT a part of the Lewis and Clark Expedition?

     a. They were to find a feasible route to the Pacific Ocean.

     b. They were to identify and report on Indian nations.

     c. They needed to catalog vegetation and map the terrain.

     d. They were to turn Indian tribes against each other.

_____   3. Which statement best describes John O'Sullivan's point of view as expressed in his *Democratic Review* article?

     a. He is a liberal concerned with the rights of the residents of Texas.

     b. He is a religious fanatic focusing only on the role of Providence in nation building.

     c. He strongly believes the superiority of European Americans entitles them to settle the rest of the continent.

     d. He is a proponent of adding slave states to the Union because of his own personal interests.

_____   4. What was the primary purpose for the American Anti-Slavery Society?

     a. William Lloyd Garrison needed an organization to back his newspaper.

     b. The Society would raise awareness of the issue of slavery and campaign for emancipation.

     c. The Society would provide women with another arena for testing societal norms.

     d. Numerous abolitionists felt the need for guidelines for civil disobedience.

_____   5. Why did the abolitionists ultimately support the Republican government?

     a. The government never resisted the movement's efforts to free slaves immediately.

     b. The Republicans allowed the parks and conservation movement to put their efforts into helping the abolitionists.

     c. The abolitionists needed government protection from the suffrage movement.

     d. The abolitionists needed to support the Union in the Civil War.

6 How is the sublime examined in American Gothic writing?

    a. The mathematical sublime is seen in the descriptions of the dark castles and eerie settings.

    b. The dynamic sublime is examined through the power of the inner workings of the mind.

    c. The fear of the self is presented as the main sublime effect within the texts.

    d. The trope of the haunted castle is used to create a mathematical sublimity response in the reader.

7. What is the difference between the mathematical and the dynamic sublime according to Kant?

    a. The mathematical sublime deals with reactions to size and the dynamic sublime with reactions to power.

    b. The mathematical sublime is experienced within the person, whereas the dynamic is a quality of the object being observed.

    c. Kant states that the mathematical and dynamic sublime occur in a sequential order.

    d. The mathematical sublime focuses on the reaction of fear, whereas the dynamic focuses on a reaction of awe.

8. How are Gothic literature and the concept of repression linked?

    a. Gothic literature deals with events that must be repressed.

    b. Gothic literature's direct focus is on repression.

    c. Through a story, Gothic literature examines actions as results of repression.

    d. Through setting and conflict, repression is exorcised from each character.

9. Which of the following would be a good example of a "tale of ratiocination"?

    a. This tale is well suited to a play about two people falling in love and living happily ever after.

    b. Usually, this tale is a story about a master criminal and the plotting of a crime.

    c. This kind of tale is best seen in a story about a young man coming of age.

    d. A poem about a beautiful vista best captures this kind of tale.

_____ 10. How were the Shakers and the Oneida community alike?

    a. Both communities believed in the concept of "Mutual Criticism" and "Complex Marriage."

    b. Both communities were religious in nature and turned to manufacturing as a means of income.

    c. Both communities were liberal in their religious beliefs and organized in a communistic fashion.

    d. Both communities suffered from lack of leadership and being ostracized by the general public.

Short Answer Questions

Answer the following questions on the lines provided.

1. How did Romanticism embody a reaction to its precursors—the Age of Reason and Puritanism?

2. Describe the concept of manifest destiny and the ramifications of a belief in such a concept.

3. Describe how the characteristics of the Gothic style of writing relate to Romanticism.

4. How did the development of psychology progress through the first half of the 19th century, and how was that progression reflected in the literature of the time?

5. How did the short story's form lend itself to the popularity of the magazines of the time?

_____

_____

_____

Summary Questions

Answer the following questions on the lines provided.

1. Summarize the argument presented in John O'Sullivan's article from the *Democratic Review.*

_____

_____

_____

_____

_____

_____

_____

2. Choose a major literary figure of the early 1800s—such as Poe, Hawthorne, Thoreau, Fuller, or another discussed in the text, and discuss his or her major contributions to literature and society.

_____

_____

_____

_____

_____

_____

3. Write a brief summary of Kant's analysis of the sublime.

_____

_____

_____

_____

_____

_____

4. What are the qualities necessary to embody the sublime according to Burke?

_____

_____

_____

_____

_____

_____

5. Describe the foundations, beliefs, and organization of one Utopian community.

_____

_____

_____

_____

_____

_____

_____

Multiple Choice Questions

Write the letter of the best answer. This exercise is continued on the next page.

_____ 1. What is one reason why mid-19th Americans were aware of the problems associated with industrialization in England?

    a. Studying industrialization was part of the mid-nineteenth century curriculum in American schools.

    b. President Lincoln often spoke about the abuses associated with industrialization.

    c. The way Charles Dickens's novels portrayed life in industrialized cities was popular with mid-19th century Americans.

    d. Henry David Thoreau's lectures familiarized Americans with the problems of industrialization.

_____ 2. What was the issue that caused a falling out between William Lloyd Garrison and Frederick Douglass?

    a. They disagreed over whether to support Lincoln's bid for the presidency.

    b. They disagreed over whether slavery should be abolished.

    c. They disagreed over whether the Constitution was a pro-slavery document.

    d. They disagreed over whether Harriet Beecher Stowe was committed to abolition.

_____ 3. How did the Know-Nothing Party get its name?

    a. Members called themselves Know-Nothings because they felt the United States should pursue an isolationist policy.

    b. Members called themselves Know-Nothings because they were anti-intellectuals.

    c. Critics named it because they thought party members were ignorant.

    d. The party was originally clandestine and members were told to say they knew nothing about it when asked.

_____ 4. What argument, put forth by Anna Ella Carroll, did Lincoln adopt to justify exercising his wartime authority?

    a. The rebellion in the South was not caused by state-wide dissention but by individual rebels whom the government needed to remove in order to restore order.

    b. The immorality of slavery nullified the legitimacy of secession.

    c. Federal properties located within the borders of secessionist states still belonged to the United States government.

    d. The views of slaves within seceding states had not been taken into consideration.

_____ 5. What policy did the Radical Republicans pursue during Reconstruction?

a. They pursued a policy of "malice toward none, and charity toward all."

b. They decided to work together with former Confederate leaders to rebuild the South.

c. They wanted to punish the South and sent in federal troops to occupy it.

d. They used the South's misfortune to enrich themselves.

_____ 6. What was the myth of the "Lost Cause"?

a. It was a dream that former slaves could be easily integrated into American society.

b. It was a belief that Lincoln could have helped the nation through Reconstruction.

c. It was a theory that slavery never existed.

d. It was a notion that the South had fought not to preserve slavery but for the noble cause of states' rights.

_____ 7. What course did the Cherokee decide to follow to hold on to their lands in the east?

a. They decided to take up arms and fight federal troops.

b. They decided to pursue legal means and declared themselves a sovereign nation.

c. They decided to practice nonviolent resistance.

d. They decided to adopt the ways of white settlers and integrate into American society.

_____ 8. Why did Cherokee Chief John Ross and many other tribe members refuse to recognize the Treaty of New Echota?

a. A small faction of the tribe, which did not represent the majority, negotiated it.

b. They felt the treaty did not offer them as much money as their land was worth.

c. It was never signed by government officials, and therefore was invalid.

d. They felt the treaty failed to recognize their status as United States citizens.

_____ 9. What was the Trail of Tears?

a. It was a Native American dance to honor dead ancestors.

b It was a secret escape route Native Americans made to get out of forts where they were held by federal troops.

c. It was a long march that Native Americans were forced to make from the East to Oklahoma.

d. It was a petition Native Americans sent to Congress calling for full citizenship.

_____ **10.** What policy toward Native Americans did Frank L. Baum advocate in his newspaper, the *Pioneer?*

    a. He advocated teaching Native Americans to govern themselves.

    b. He advocated total extermination of Native Americans.

    c. He advocated giving Native Americans better land so they could grow their own crops.

    d. He advocated enlisting Native Americans into the U.S. Army.

Short Answer Questions

Answer the following questions on the lines provided.

1. How did supporters of slavery justify their position?

_____
_____
_____
_____

2. What arguments does Harriet Beecher Stowe make in her letter to William Lloyd Garrison to persuade him to reconcile with Frederick Douglass?

_____
_____
_____

3. What were some reasons for the rise of the nativist movement in the 1840s?

_____
_____
_____
_____

4. What was the right of "popular sovereignty" and how did it contribute to increasing divisions among Americans in the years leading up to the Civil War?

_____
_____
_____
_____

5. What are some ways entrepreneurs found to make money during the California Gold Rush?

_____

_____

_____

_____

Summary Questions

Answer the following questions on the lines provided.

1. What were some of the events leading up to secession?

_____

_____

_____

_____

_____

_____

_____

_____

2. Explain the situation of former African American slaves in the South at the end of Reconstruction.

_____

_____

_____

_____

_____

_____

_____

_____

3. Explain the motivations that fueled the westward expansion in the mid-19th century.

_____

_____

_____

_____

_____

4. Summarize how Andrew Jackson justified his policy of relocating Native Americans in the West.

_____

_____

_____

_____

_____

5. Explain why the Ghost Dance religion appealed so strongly to Native American tribes on the Great Plains and why many U.S. government officials feared it.

_____

_____

_____

_____

_____

Multiple Choice Questions

Write the letter of the best answer. This exercise is continued on the next page.

_____ 1. Who was known as a "trust buster"?

    a. Franklin D. Roosevelt

    b. Samuel Gompers

    c. W. E. B. DuBois

    d. Theodore Roosevelt

_____ 2. Which Amendment allowed African American men to vote?

    a. 12th

    b. 15th

    c. 14th

    d. 19th

_____ 3. What is _Art Deco_?

    a. a technique of photography

    b. an educational movement

    c. an activity at Hull-House

    d. a style of decorative and industrial arts

_____ 4. Which college was first committed to education for both sexes and all races?

    a. Rockford Seminary

    b. Oberlin College

    c. University of Pennsylvania

    d. Troy Seminary

_____ 5. What entertainment most thrilled tourists at the 1893 World's Fair?

    a. first videos

    b. trolley ride

    c. Ferris wheel

    d. elevator rides

_____ 6. Who spoke out against Booker T. Washington's approach to "the Negro problem"?

    a. Eugene Debs

    b. W. E. B. DuBois

    c. Jane Addams

    d. Susan B. Anthony

_____ 7. Which of the following two women were journalists?

    a. Ida B. Wells and Rebecca Latimer Felton

    b. Sojourner Truth and Tillie Olsen

    c. Lillian Hellman and Florence Kelley

    d. Ellen Gates Starr and Jane Addams

_____ 8. For what was Margaret Sanger well known?

    a. medicine on the reservation

    b. birth control

    c. Settlement House movement

    d. Red Cross

_____ 9. Who was Lewis Hine?

    a. sweatshop inspector

    b. factory inspector

    c. reform-minded teacher

    d. social-activist photographer

_____ 10. Who founded the Red Cross?

    a. William LeBaron Jenney

    b. Clara Barton

    c. Susan La Flesche

    d. Emma Willard

Short Answer Questions

Answer the following questions on the lines provided.

1. Explain the political reform of *recall*.

_____

_____

_____

_____

2. How did Hull-House serve immigrants?

_____

_____

_____

_____

3. What did child doffers do?

    _____

    _____

    _____

4. On what did Sojourner Truth and Frances Harper disagree?

    _____

    _____

    _____

5. What is the "Anthony Amendment"?

    _____

    _____

    _____

Summary Questions

Answer the following questions on the lines provided.

1. Summarize why the metal frame and safety elevator were important to the development of the skyscraper.

    _____

    _____

    _____

    _____

    _____

2. Summarize Samuel Gompers's response to trusts.

    _____

    _____

    _____

    _____

    _____

3. Summarize the ideas of Booker T. Washington in response to
   "the Negro problem."

   _____

   _____

   _____

   _____

   _____

   _____

   _____

4. Summarize the evolution of educational opportunities for
   American women.

   _____

   _____

   _____

   _____

   _____

   _____

   _____

5. Summarize how the debate for suffrage changed after the Civil War.

   _____

   _____

   _____

   _____

   _____

   _____

   _____

Multiple Choice Questions

Write the letter of the best answer. This exercise is continued on the next page.

_____ 1. The primary purpose of Jim Crow laws was to do which of the following?

    a. deny blacks the vote

    b. segregate schools

    c. maintain white supremacy

    d. force a black migration north

_____ 2. In his essay, Alain Locke states that the New Negro is someone who

    a. should seek reparations for slavery

    b. should create his own identity

    c. is an artist or intellectual

    d. is superior to whites

_____ 3. Much of African-American music has characteristics that arose from which of the following?

    a. West African call-and-response singing

    b. West African drumming and ritual

    c. Non-Christian religious ceremonies

    d. New Orleans blues singing

_____ 4. The Red Scare in the United States almost immediately followed what significant world event?

    a. The rise of union organizing

    b. An influx of immigrants to America

    c. The Palmer Raids

    d. The Bolshevik Revolution in Russia

_____ 5. Who were the Wobblies?

    a. They were Russian extremists

    b. They were labor organizers

    c. They were anarchists

    d. They were World War I veterans

_____ 6. A flapper was

    a. a 1920s dance craze

    b. a type of bootleg liquor

    c. a liberated woman of the 1920s

    d. a popular film star of the 1920s

_____ 7. The forerunners of today's paperback books were the
   a. pulps
   b. silents
   c. flappers
   d. magazines

_____ 8. The "Lost Generation" was a group of expatriate artists in the 1920s who lived in
   a. Russia
   b. Paris
   c. Harlem
   d. Chicago

_____ 9. Radio helped create American consumer society because in the 1920s it
   a. began broadcasting sports
   b. was very inexpensive
   c. created a national identity
   d. began accepting advertising

_____ 10. Henry Ford revolutionized manufacturing when he began to use
   a. the Model T
   b. mechanization
   c. the assembly line
   d. efficiency experts

Short Answer Questions

Answer the following questions on the lines provided.

1. When the Great Depression hit, what conditions led most Americans to lose the savings they had put in the bank?

_____

_____

_____

2. How does Robert Benchley's satire attack the methods used during the Red Scare to find and destroy dissidents?

_____

_____

_____

3. What are two significant events that led to the liberation of women in
    the 1920s?

    _____

    _____

    _____

    _____

4. How did Frederick Taylor's ideas dehumanize factory workers?

    _____

    _____

    _____

    _____

5. In what way are blues and jazz music related to West African music?

    _____

    _____

    _____

    _____

Summary Questions

Answer the following questions on the lines provided.

1. What effect did buying stock on margin have on the Crash of 1929?

    _____

    _____

    _____

    _____

    _____

2. What was the relationship between America's entry into World War I and the attitudes that led to the Red Scare?

_____

_____

_____

_____

_____

_____

3. How did the popularity of the automobile increase Americans' sense of alienation?

_____

_____

_____

_____

_____

_____

4. What was the "double consciousness" blacks in the South had to learn to live with in the 1920s? Why was it necessary?

_____

_____

_____

_____

_____

_____

5. What were two conditions that led to the Dust Bowl of the thirties?

_____

_____

_____

_____

_____

_____

Multiple Choice Questions

Write the letter of the best answer. This exercise is continued on the next page.

_____ 1. Who convinced President Roosevelt to stop discrimination in war industries?

    a. Colin Powell

    b. A. Phillip Randolph

    c. Dorrie Miller

    d. Benjamin Davis Jr.

_____ 2. During which war did all troops fight in desegregated units for the first time in modern warfare?

    a. World War II

    b. Vietnam War

    c. Korean War

    d. First Gulf War

_____ 3. Which event prompted the U.S. to enter World War II?

    a. the Japanese attack on Pearl Harbor

    b. Hitler's persecution of the Jews

    c. the desire to acquire natural resources in Russia

    d. the threat of invasion on American soil

_____ 4. N. Scott Momaday uses what postmodern technique in *The Way to Rainy Mountain?*

    a. dislocation

    b. contextualism

    c. creating own universe

    d. unusual juxtapositions

_____ 5. Which pair below includes one person who wrote about the other and who was born in the same state?

    a. Saul Bellow and Allen Ginsberg

    b. Toni Morrison and Cristina Garcia

    c. Alice Walker and Flannery O'Connor

    d. Martin Luther King and Henry David Thoreau

_____ 6. Which is a hallmark of postmodern architecture?

    a. heavily ornamental design

    b. melding of periods and styles

    c. the scale of buildings to people is disproportionate

    d. blends into the surrounding landscape

_____ 7. Conglomerates began influencing press coverage significantly during what decade?

    a. 1950s

    b. 1990s

    c. 1980s

    d. 1970s

_____ 8. *Blackboard Jungle* linked what two aspects of youth culture during the 1950s?

    a. Sitcoms and pop charts

    b. middle class life and school

    c. cars and drive-ins

    d. juvenile delinquents and rock and roll

_____ 9. Which of the following was influenced by jazz?

    A. Saul Bellow in *Augie March*

    B. Flannery O'Connor in "A Good Man Is Hard to Find"

    C. Jewish writers of the 1950s

    D. Beats of the 1950s

_____ 10. Which statement describes modernism better than postmodernism?

    a. It uses strange juxtapositions in architecture

    b. It looks more toward the past than toward the future

    c. It looks more toward the future than toward the past

    d. Dislocation is a key characteristic

Short Answer Questions

Answer the following questions on the lines provided.

1. Why did African American soldiers return home dissatisfied after World War II?

_____

_____

_____

2. Why did Senator Margaret Chase Smith address Congress in 1950?

_____

_____

_____

3. How did television hurt Joseph McCarthy?

_____

_____

_____

_____

4. What are press pools?

_____

_____

_____

_____

5. How did the press coverage of Vietnam change after 1968?

_____

_____

_____

Summary Questions

Answer the following questions on the lines provided.

1. Explain why increasing numbers of African Americans in the military during the Vietnam War and afterward might be seen as a sign of discrimination.

_____

_____

_____

_____

_____

_____

_____

2. Explain how conglomerates affect news coverage?

_____

_____

_____

_____

_____

_____

3. Compare and contrast three strains of resistance in the Civil Rights movement.

_____

_____

_____

_____

_____

_____

4. In what ways were the 1950s a time of conformity and also a time of innovation?

_____

_____

_____

_____

_____

_____

5. In what ways is youth culture today similar to youth culture of the 1950s and 1960s?

_____

_____

_____

_____

_____

∽ UNIT 1 ∾

Multiple Choice Questions

1.	a	6.	a
2.	c	7.	a
3.	b	8.	c
4.	d	9.	d
5.	b	10.	c

Short Answer Questions

1. **Possible answer:** The white settlers at first tried to appease their Native American neighbors, but their beliefs that they were a superior people to the Native Americans indicate that they were going to claim rights to the lands whether the Native Americans liked it or not. This superior attitude often led to conflict between the two peoples. The disregard for the Native Americans' rights demonstrates the settlers' belief in their supremacy over the native culture and in their right to claim the land as their own. Finally, the settlers' behavior in trying to convert the "savages" shows an arrogant belief that only they have the one true religion.

2. **Possible answer:** The ethnocentricity of explorers led them to make many sweeping generalizations about the native cultures. They often concluded that these people had no religion, no organization of society, and no value as human beings because they were different from the explorers. By describing the natives as "less than" or as the "other," the explorers gave themselves and their colleagues license to destroy civilizations and to enslave other humans just because they were different.

3. **Possible answer:** These songs and tales were a means of communicating the hope of freedom in an enslaved society. They also provided a means of expressing cultural beliefs as well as sharing the common sense of the enslaved people. For these reasons, these spirituals and tales provided a sharp contrast to the cruelty of the slaveholders.

4. **Possible answer:** The Native American oral tradition provided a means for the community to connect to the supernatural, to preserve the cultural heritage, to celebrate the culture and monumental events, and to express beliefs and values. The oral tradition was a vital part of everyday life within the culture.

5. **Possible answer:** To experience the text, we read a written version of a work that was originally meant to be performed orally. In addition, we must read an English translation of the written record of the oral work. Finally, we do not necessarily understand the cultural traditions from which the work comes nor what that work celebrates. Thus, we add a further layer of removal from the text. To bridge the gap in understanding, we can familiarize ourselves with the cultural values and beliefs of the work's originating culture and possibly examine a variety of translations to gather a fuller sense of meaning.

Summary Questions

1. **Possible answer:** Origin tales and creation myths are considered true history of the beginnings of the earth. Fictional tales, such as trickster tales, express cultural beliefs and values. Songs provide a means of communication with the supernatural and form an integral part of ceremonial life.

2. **Possible answer:** The earth was soft and wet when the Great Buzzard came to prepare the world for the animals. Because the buzzard's wings were huge, they made impressions in the earth as he flew. When he was tired, his sagging wings carved out valleys. Mountains were made when he lifted his wings and rose up.

3. **Possible answer:** Songs serve as a means of communicating with the supernatural and are vital parts of ceremonial culture. They are sung, as this song was originally intended, before entering into battle as a sort of prayer. In addition, songs provide a vehicle for passing on a cultural heritage. In this song, readers understand that the threat to life is taken into account and that the family and its suffering is highly regarded in the culture.

4. **Possible answer:** Africans were brought to work on the plantations because the natives of the islands and the continent were not able to withstand the harsh treatment inflicted on them by the Europeans. Also, the natives knew the country well, so they often escaped. The enslaved Africans were also the receivers of harsh treatment. They were often beaten and were expected to perform extraordinary amounts of work. In addition, their cultural and familial ties were either denigrated or ignored.

5. **Possible answer:** Ten years before the letter was written, Smith was taken captive by Powhatan, Pocahontas's father. Smith lived with the Native Americans for six weeks, and then he was to be executed. However,

Pocahontas saved his life by putting herself in danger and assisting in obtaining his safe return to Jamestown. When he returned to Jamestown, he found the settlers sick and starving. The Native Americans took pity on them and gave them food, which was often delivered by Pocahontas.

∽UNIT 2∾

Multiple Choice Questions

1. c   6. d
2. d   7. b
3. c   8. a
4. b   9. b
5. a   10. d

Short Answer Questions

1. **Possible answer:** Puritan women were viewed as essentially inferior to men in all matters outside the home, especially religious matters. However, they were well schooled in practical matters having to do with running their homes and their husband's businesses. They were also seen by ministers as valuable life partners who should be cherished.

2. **Possible answer:** Because the Puritans saw all acts on Earth as coming from a divine power, they believed that the Salem Witch Trials had been a punishment for their bad prior acts as well as a challenge to their faith. One of their best qualities was that of self-examination, which they put to use after the trials. This introspection led to the establishment of a day to ask forgiveness.

3. **Possible answer:** John Edwards's writing was characterized by persuasive methods such as the logical, elegant construction of arguments to prove his points—even though his points were emotional and psychological in nature. His sermonizing was undramatic, but his words held such force that he was a powerful speaker nonetheless.

4. **Possible answer:** John Locke wrote about the concept of "natural rights," including the right to life, liberty, and ownership of property. He held that if governments prevented citizens from these natural rights, citizens had the right to revolt. The Bible also supported independence with tales of rulers who were unfair.

5. **Possible answer:** While Crèvecoeur believed there was almost nothing wrong with America or Americans, he tended to ignore people's narrow-mindedness with regard to slavery and

ethnicity. Franklin knew there was sectionalism developing in the new country and that people harbored mixed feelings about England.

Summary Questions

1. **Possible answer:** In some ways, the negative view of the Puritans is correct. They were rigid in their behavior and beliefs. They were always examining their own behavior, however, which implies openness. They also enjoyed the benefits of material wealth, seeing it as their just reward. In addition, they valued education and reading.

2. **Possible answer:** The intellectualism of the Puritans was evident in many ways: They established a printing press, free public grammar schools, and Harvard College. They also insisted that everyone in the community support the college. In addition, their governmental model of elections and town meetings suggested that they were thoughtful, serious-minded people.

3. **Possible answer:** The Puritans saw captivity as both a challenge and a punishment. Captivity was more intense than their daily lives, but it was on the same spectrum as a divinely-driven phenomenon. As seen in Mary Rowlandson's narrative, God alternately punishes and challenges his children. The struggle of literal captivity mirrored the psychic captivity of the mortal soul.

4. **Possible answer:** Jonathan Edwards symbolized the end of one period and the beginning of another period. A traditional Puritan, he spoke to American conflicts that occurred between settlers and newcomers as well as farmers and merchants. With logic, he convinced people that accepting God was the only hope for their salvation. Ironically, however, Edwards was finally rejected as people began to expand their personal definitions of what constituted religious practice.

5. **Possible answer:** The most vocal and powerful proponent of revolution was Thomas Paine, who deeply believed that the colonies must separate from England. Both *Common Sense* and *The American Crisis* served as the inspiration for many colonists to rally to the cause. In addition, the great leader George Washington should be credited for his actions in mobilizing the country to fight. There were also lesser but notable female figures who inspired others with their valor and determination.

ANSWER KEY

∽UNIT 3∾

Multiple Choice Questions

1. b	6. b
2. d	7. a
3. c	8. c
4. b	9. b
5. d	10. b

Short Answer Questions

1. **Possible answer:** Instead of denigrating the self, Romanticism celebrated it. Romanticism reacted to Puritanism and the Age of Reason by celebrating the wildness of the emotions and the importance of the individual. In addition, Romanticism viewed the emotions as more important or advanced than reason.

2. **Possible answer:** Manifest destiny was a belief that Americans had a God-given right to claim the land for themselves. This concept also advocated the responsibility of the Americans to spread their advanced means of government, namely democracy, to people who could not rule themselves. In effect, these people were the Native Americans and Mexicans that held the land that the Americans wanted. As a result of believing in this concept, Americans saw themselves as morally and intellectually superior to the Native Americans and Mexicans. Therefore, they felt justified in taking what belonged to these peoples. In the end, the implementation of manifest destiny nearly wiped out the Native American culture by its horrifying treatment of fellow human beings.

3. **Possible answer:** Like Romanticism, the Gothic style reflects a reaction to the rationalism of the Age of Reason. It emphasizes the imagination and the individual, although in a darker, more sinister way. Emotion is an important element in both Gothic and romantic writing, but Gothic writing examines emotions such as fear, terror, mistrust, suspicion, greed, and unhappiness.

4. **Possible answer:** In the first half of the 19th century, people perceived the mentally ill as threats to themselves and society. As they began to understand mental illness as a sickness, the treatment began to improve. With the examination of mental illness came the examinations of personality traits and behaviors. These examinations were echoed in the Romantics' exploration and celebration of the self and the emotions. The Gothic writers took the examination to the dark side of the mind, looking for essential truths in the unknown chambers of the personality.

5. **Possible answer:** Because the purpose of the literary magazines of the time was to sell large quantities to a middle-class audience, the short story form was perfect. The length suited an average reader because a big commitment of time was not needed to complete the reading. In addition, the compelling nature of the tale did not suffer because it was based on a plot just like a novel, only shorter.

Summary Questions

1. **Possible answer:** O'Sullivan argues that people need to simply accept the annexation of Texas because it is God's plan for America to spread across the country and take control of the land.

2. **Possible answer:** Answers will vary depending on the chosen literary figure, but students should include the main works discussed and the person's contribution to society. Sample answer: Edgar Allan Poe showed the intricacies of the human mind by weaving it into a strange, mysterious, and compelling tale. His plots gave a story line to the same kind of research into human emotions that scientists of the time were exploring. Such powerful stories opened up paths through the human mind in ways any reader could understand.

3. **Possible answer:** Kant believed that the sublime took two forms: mathematical and dynamic. Mathematical sublimity deals with our reactions to size and infinitude. Dynamic sublimity deals with our reactions to power. Kant also believed that the concept of sublimity resided within the person perceiving and not in the object being perceived.

4. **Possible answer:** Burke believed that to embody sublimity an object must possess elements that elicit astonishment, fear, and awe. Additionally, the object of awe must have power and it must have an element of the unknown in order to embody the sublime.

5. **Possible answer:** Answers will vary depending on the community chosen. Sample answer: The Brook Farm community was established by George Ripley and his wife Sophia as a haven for intellectuals to connect and prosper in a pleasant community setting. The community was closely linked to the literary world of the time and to the Transcendentalists. The community thrived for several years, but when Ripley began following Fourierism, members became unhappy and soon left. Ultimately, the community failed in 1847.

UNIT 4

Multiple Choice Questions

1. a   6. d
2. c   7. b
3. d   8. a
4. a   9. c
5. c   10. b

Short Answer Questions

1. **Possible answer:** Supporters of slavery used religion, biology, and social issues to justify their position. They also contrasted the "hireling" system of labor in the industrialized North, which left people unemployed and underpaid, with the Southern plantation system, which guaranteed work for all in return for lifelong care including housing, food, and medical attention.

2. **Possible answer:** She writes that Douglass is not bitter or vengeful over their differences. His change of sentiments seems to come out of real conviction. He can defend his positions, which show he didn't just adopt them from someone else. There should be room within the abolitionist cause for people of different opinions, and she hopes that Douglass will keep silent on the subject in the future so as not to make the divisions even worse.

3. **Possible answer:** Many Americans felt that new waves of immigrants threatened their jobs because the newcomers were willing to work for lower wages. Many of the newcomers were Catholics and there was a history of anti-Catholic sentiments among Protestants dating back to the early Protestant settlers who emigrated to America to escape persecution from the Catholic Church. Protestant Americans feared Catholics may undermine democracy because of their loyalty to the Pope.

4. **Possible answer:** Popular sovereignty was the right of residents of new territories to decide for themselves whether their state would be free or slave. It reopened the question of slavery in new states, which had been laid to rest in the Missouri Compromise of 1820, leading pro- and anti-slavery settlers to violence in Bleeding Kansas.

5. **Possible answer:** They identified goods and services needed by miners and found ways to provide them. Enterprising women ran boarding houses, cooked meals, and washed miners' clothes. Levi Strauss made sturdy pants with

riveted pockets for miners. Henry Wells and William Fargo founded the Wells Fargo Bank to provide miners with banking services.

Summary Questions

1. **Possible answer:** In 1854, Congress passed the Kansas-Nebraska Act giving residents the right of popular sovereignty, threatening the balance of power between existing free and slave states. People around the country followed escalating violence in "Bleeding Kansas" between pro- and anti-slavery residents closely. The Dred Scott ruling—that slaves were not legally citizens and therefore could not sue for their freedom in free states—further enflamed passions. Abolitionist John Brown's raid on a federal arsenal at Harper's Ferry further divided the nation. Many Southerners saw Lincoln's election as a threat, although he had declared he had no intention of ending slavery in states where it already existed.

2. **Possible answer:** They benefited from many of the efforts of the Freedmen's Bureau which provided rations and medical care, helped them negotiate labor contracts, and built and financed schools for African American children. However, they were left at the mercy of Black Codes, laws passed in many Southern states to limit their right to work, own property, move about freely, possess firearms, and vote. They were also subject to violence from the Ku Klux Klan, and from white mobs in cities that felt threatened by African Americans moving to urban areas and competing for jobs and housing.

3. **Possible answer:** After gold was discovered in California, many people set out to strike it rich out West. Irish immigrants fleeing the potato famine were drawn to California. So were many Chinese immigrants who hoped to send money home from "Gold Mountain." Immigrants from all over the world went out West seeking opportunity. Newspapermen were drawn by the adventurous freewheeling life in California. The city of San Francisco became a bustling cultural center that drew many. Some people took advantage of the Homestead Act to settle the Great Plains on free land. Others, such as the Mormons, went out West seeking religious freedom, and settled in Utah.

4. **Possible answer:** Jackson said civilization was moving westward beyond anyone's control. Due to events beyond the government's control, Native Americans were unhappy on their old lands. Their existence would be guaranteed by moving west. He pointed out that the country's European ancestors had once left behind everything familiar to emigrate to America. Many Americans were now leaving behind all

that was familiar to seek fortune and opportunity out West. The government was offering Native Americans a great deal—one that many Americans would be happy to accept, namely to pay them for their land, to pay the expense of the journey West, to give them new land and support.

5. **Possible answer:** The Ghost Dance religion appealed to Native American tribes on the Great Plains because it prophesied that a time was coming when Native Americans would recover their land and their old way of life. White settlers would be swallowed up by the earth and the buffalo and other wildlife over-hunted by white settlers would reappear. Many U.S. government officials feared the Ghost Dance religion because they thought it would incite a new round of Native American uprisings.

UNIT 5

Multiple Choice Questions

1. d	6. b
2. b	7. a
3. d	8. b
4. b	9. d
5. c	10. b

Short Answer Questions

1. **Possible answer:** Recall allowed voters to decide if an elected official should or should not fulfill his full term.

2. **Possible answer:** Hull-House was a Settlement House offering daycare, lectures on sanitation and parenting, reading classes, and "uplifting" entertainment (painting, music, drama), among other services.

3. **Possible answer:** They changed bobbins and mended broken thread in textile factories.

4. **Possible answer:** Truth thought the suffragist movement should continue to fight for universal suffrage, while Harper thought the right of African American men to vote should be secured first.

5. **Possible answer:** It was a proposal presented to Congress by Elizabeth Cady Stanton and Susan B. Anthony in 1878. It did not pass and was reintroduced for the next 41 years until eventually it became the 19th Amendment, a U.S. Constitutional Amendment that allows women to vote.

Summary Questions

1. **Possible answer:** The metal frame allowed buildings to be built higher without thick walls, because the frame was strong enough to carry great weight. The elevator allowed people to travel vertically much farther than they could do comfortably by climbing stairs. Without safe elevators, people would not be able to inhabit skyscrapers. Without the metal frame, most buildings would probably be no higher than 10 stories because the thickness of the walls would severely limit interior space and natural light.

2. **Possible answer:** Gompers did not want to destroy trusts. He thought consolidation was inevitable. He believed that trade unions should also consolidate and form a counter-institution to strengthen labor's interests.

3. **Possible answer:** He believed that African Americans should accommodate a hostile society and train for vocations such as domestics, mechanics, or carpenters. His philosophy was called "gradualism." He did not advocate fighting for civil rights immediately.

4. **Possible answer:** First, reformers fought for elementary and secondary educational opportunities for girls. For example, Emma Willard asked for New York state funds to open Troy Female Seminary in 1819. She argued that girls should be allowed to "be of use" to themselves and others. She did not receive state funds but raised private funds to open her school. Seminaries also opened in the South for white girls, while African American teachers opened schools for African American students, until doing so was outlawed.

   Next, colleges began permitting females to attend classes, beginning with Oberlin in 1833. After that, some women trained to be teachers, social workers, nurses, doctors, and even engineers.

5. **Possible answer:** The question arose after the Civil War about whether suffragists should focus attention on voting rights of African American men before continuing the fight for women. This question caused some division of thought as well as some racist arguments as educated white women sometimes compared themselves favorably to uneducated African American people and immigrants. After the 15th Amendment was passed in 1870, which did not include women but allowed African American men to vote, all suffragists focused on universal suffrage and worked to pass the 19th Amendment.

∽UNIT 6∾

Multiple Choice Questions

1.	c	6.	c
2.	b	7.	a
3.	a	8.	b
4.	d	9.	d
5.	b	10.	c

Short Answer Questions

1. **Possible answer:** Bank savings then were not insured by the government, and banks had invested the deposits in stocks.

2. **Possible answer:** He shows how a perfectly innocent and reasonable statement can be twisted to make a person appear traitorous and guilty, even though they are not.

3. **Possible answer:** Women had worked in factories during World War I and the country was rich and they had money.

4. **Possible answer:** He broke down every movement of a task and timed it so it could be done as quickly as possible, without consideration for the person doing the job.

5. **Possible answer:** All involve a type of call-and-response and both improvise in harmony and rhythm.

Summary Questions

1. **Possible answer:** Buying stock on margin meant that most of the worth of the stock was in the form of a loan, or was not real money. Companies that issued the stock therefore thought they had more investment than they actually did.

2. **Possible answer:** No dissent against America's entry into the war was permitted, and those who did dissent were considered traitors or were persecuted.

3. **Possible answer:** It increased Americans' sense of rootlessness, it led to growth of isolating suburbs where neighbors rarely got to know each other, and to long commutes between home and job.

4. **Possible answer:** They had to wear a mask of submission while restraining and not expressing their feelings of humiliation and rage they harbored.

5. **Possible answer:** Unwise farming practices that led to out-of-control soil erosion and a prolonged drought led to the Dust Bowl.

∽UNIT 7∾

Multiple Choice Questions

1.	b	6.	b
2.	c	7.	c
3.	a	8.	d
4.	d	9.	d
5.	c	10.	c

Short Answer Questions

1. **Possible answer:** They had fought bravely in the war and been treated as equals by grateful Europeans, but at home they were treated as second-class citizens.

2. **Possible answer:** She was afraid of how negatively the oppressive atmosphere of McCarthyism would affect the country. She was also concerned about the blatant disregard for the constitutional right to the freedom of speech and to trial by jury, and so she spoke out against it.

3. **Possible answer:** Viewers could see that McCarthy unfairly attacked people, so viewers eventually turned against McCarthy.

4. **Possible answer:** Press pools include press members who accompanied troops during the Gulf War[s]. The press pools allowed the press access to the military but limited their access to other perspectives.

5. **Possible answer:** The press became more detached from military objectives and more critical of the war, reflecting popular discontent.

Summary Questions

1. **Possible answer:** During the Vietnam War, African Americans were drafted while white Americans often obtained deferments to finish their education. This inequality showed that whites had more educational and economic opportunities in civilian society than did blacks. It seemed unfair that African Americans were asked to carry the largest burden in an unpopular war, especially since they had not achieved their civil rights at home.

2. **Possible answer:** Conglomerates are not journalistic organizations, but they control the media and much of today's journalism. Conglomerations have diverse interests such as entertainment, amusement parks, sports, appliances, etc. Their primary purpose is to make money. Therefore, they are willing to compromise in-depth journalistic coverage in

order to gain wide viewership and high-paying sponsors. They favor advertising techniques such as repetition and fast pacing over critical coverage. News is made to fit a predetermined story script.

3. **Possible answer:** First, Martin Luther King Jr.'s nonviolent resistance, which sought to integrate society, drew inspiration from Christianity, Thoreau, and Gandhi. Second, militant resistance sought separate African American communities, and was influenced by Black Muslims and led by Malcolm X. Third, militant resistance sought political and economic goals, and was influenced by Marxism and ghetto realities and led by the Black Panther Party and SNCC. All three strains sought equality and fairness for African Americans. They differed in the means, however, (nonviolent vs. violent) and the end results (integrated society vs. separate spheres of power).

4. **Possible answer:** Conformity could be found on television, which aired sitcoms that highlighted ideal white middle-class families that upheld the status quo. Conformity could also be found in the literary establishment, which primarily acknowledged literature written by white males. Finally, conformity was seen in the pop chart's uninspiring, conservative music. Innovation could be found in "youth culture" which celebrated rock and roll music. It was seen in films such as *Rebel without A Cause,* which explored issues of alienation; it was also in Beat culture, which criticized American culture. Innovation was part of the Civil Rights movement, which fought for justice and, finally, innovation was seen in emerging new voices in literature including southern writing, Jewish writing, and the Beats' writing.

5. **Possible answer:** Young people today live in a consumer society and a time of conformity, just as the young people in the 1950s. They listen to music that evolved from African American rhythm and blues. Advertising and postmodern economics encourage young people today to consume and to tailor their goals toward economic success (goals similar to the ones of the youth of the 1950s). However, campus activists today see through "productless" advertising and have organized protests similar to the protests of the 1960s. Young people today also enjoy reading literature written by authors of diverse backgrounds. Young people in the 1950s and the 1960s were only beginning to discover alternative authors and more often read the established authors.

INDEX

ACKNOWLEDGMENTS

Acknowledgments

44 *The Salem Witchcraft Papers,* Vol. 1, p. 29, from the records of the Court of Oyer and Terminer, 1692. Property of the Supreme Judicial Court, Division of Archives and Records Preservation. On deposit at the Peabody Essex Museum, Salem, Massachusetts.
71 "George Ripley's Letter of Resignation." From the American Transcendentalism Web, at <http://www.vcu.edu/transcendentalism/ideas/letter.html>.
85 "Letter from Harriet Beecher Stowe," from *The Life and Writings of Frederick Douglass,* Volume II: Pre-Civil War Decade 1850–1860, Philip S. Foner, ed. (International Publishers, 1950).
99 "Letter from Chief John Ross" (Sept. 28, 1836), from *The Papers of Chief John Ross,* Vol. 1, 1807–1839, by Gary E. Moulton, ed. (University of Oklahoma Press, 1985). Reprinted by permission.
112 "Declaration of Sentiments," from *A History of Woman Suffrage,* Vol. 1, by Elizabeth Cady Stanton, (Rochester, NY: Fowler and Wells, 1889), pages 70–71. Internet History Sourcebooks Project at <http://www.fordham.edu/halsall/mod/Senecafalls.html>.
149 "The Great Dust Storm," from "Dust Storm Disaster," by Woody Guthrie. Lyrics and music by Woody Guthrie. TRO Copyright © 1960 (renewed), 1963 (renewed) Ludlow Music, Inc., New York, NY. Used by permission.
165 "I Have a Dream," by Martin Luther King. Copyright © 1963 (renewed 1991 by the estate of Martin Luther King). Reprinted by arrangement with the Heirs to the Estate of Martin Luther King, Jr., c/o Writers House, LLC, as agent for the proprietor.
166 Excerpt from *The Autobiography of Malcolm X,* by Malcolm X with the assistance of Alex Haley. Copyright © 1964 by Alex Haley and Malcolm X. Copyright © 1965 by Alex Haley and Betty Shabazz. Used by permission of Random House, Inc.

Photo Credits

47 "Join or Die," woodcut by Ben Franklin. LOC: Prints and Photographs Division (P&P) (LC-USZ62-9701); **48** "A.S. Adams," LOC: P&P (LC-USZ62-112534); **60** "Canyon of Yellowstone" by Thomas Moran. LOC: P&P (LC-USZC4-4411); **66** 1841 *New England Anti-Slavery Society Almanac* cover, Old Sturbridge Village; **67** "The Bloomer Costume," LOC: P&P (LC-USZ62-970); **73** "The Symbolical Head," LOC: P&P (LC-USZ62-100747); **84** Photo: "Mathew Brady at Army of the Potomac headquarters." LOC: P&P (LC-B8171-2433); **88** "Dred Scott," LOC: P&P (LC-USZ62-5092); **93** 3 sketches by Daniel Jenks: "Sunday," LOC: P&P (LC-USZ62-128887); "Cherokee Pass, Rocky Mountains," LOC: P&P (LC-USZ62-128886); "Camp 90, DeCasure Creek," LOC: P&P (LC-USZ62-128893); **94** "Pilgrims on the Plains" by Theo. R. Davis. LOC: P&P (LC-USZ62-133213); **96** Photo: "Train with Indians in the Background," LOC: American Memory Collection: Buckaroos in Paradise: Ranching Culture in Northern Nevada, 1945–1982. Call Number NV9-CF26-9; Digital ID afc96ran 46050; **100** "The Ghost Dance by the Ogallala Sioux at Pine Ridge Agency" by Frederic Remington. LOC: P&P (LC-USZ62-99404); **105** Cartoon: "Election Day!" LOC: P&P (LC-USZ62-51821). Copyright by E.W. Gustin, 1909. J72583 U.S. Copyright Office; **109** Photo: "Rear View of Tenement, 134 1/2 Thompson Street, New York City" by Lewis Hines. LOC: P&P (LC-USZ62-93116); **114** Photo: "The First Picket Line - College Day in the Picket Line," LOC: P&P (LC-USZ62-31799); **116** Photo: "Mrs. Lucy Libertine" by Lewis Hines. LOC: P&P (LC-USZ62-26527); **117** Photo: "Woolworth Building at Night, NYC." LOC: P&P (LC-USZ62-106874). Copyright William Townand (?), J181147 U.S. Copyright Office; **118** Photo: "Fuller Building," LOC: P&P (LC-USZ62-74593). Copyright Charles L. Ritzmann; **122** Photo: "Young Doffer Boy" by Lewis Hines. LOC: P&P (LC-DIG-nclc-0278); **123** Photo: "Doffer Boys in Bibb Mill #1" by Lewis Hines. LOC: P&P (LC-DIG-nclc-05400); **123** Photo: "Young Sweeper and Doffer, Roanoke (Va.) Cotton Mills" by Lewis Hines. LOC: P&P (LC-USZ62-19573); **127** Photo: "Duke Ellington" by Gordon Parks. LOC: P&P: Farm Security Administration/Office of War Information Photograph Collection (LC-USW3-023947-C); **128** Photo: "Drinking Fountain on County Courthouse Lawn" by John Vachon. LOC: P&P (LC-USZ62-100414); **136** Photo: "A French Departure Trench Just Before Zero Hour," LOC: P&P (LC-USZ62-93510). U.S. Copyright Office, No. W116; **140** Cartoon: "Step By Step," from Red Scare, An Image Database at the Newman Library, Baruch College, CUNY. Originally published 11/01/19 in *New York Evening Telegram;* **141** Photo: "Charleston at the Capitol," LOC: P&P (LC-USZ62-93721); **144** Photo: "Young Woman Tuning a Radio," LOC: P&P: National Photo Company Collection. (LC-USZ62-108097); **148** Photo: "Jobless Men Keep Going," U.S. National Archives and Records Administration; **149** Photo: "Dust Bowl Farm. Coldwater District, North of Dalhart, Texas, 1938" by Dorothea Lange. LOC: P&P: Farm Security Administration/Office of War Information Photograph Collection (LC-USZ62-130634); **154** Photo: "Gunnar Myrdal" by G. Paul Bishop; **165** Photo: "MLK and Malcom X, 1964" by Marion S. Trikosko. LOC: P&P: *U.S. News & World Report Magazine* Photograph Collection. (LC-USZ6-1847); **171** Photo: "Renaissance Center" by Mary Ann Sullivan, Bluffton University.